D0914475

The Closed Frontier

Studies in American Literary Tragedy

The Closed Frontier

Studies in American Literary Tragedy

HAROLD P. SIMONSON
University of Washington

Holt, Rinehart and Winston, Inc.

New York   Chicago   San Francisco   Atlanta
Dallas   Montreal   Toronto   London   Sydney

Acknowledgments

Portions of this book have appeared in slightly different form in the following periodicals:
    Chapter 2   ("Frederick Jackson Turner: Frontier History as Art") from *The Antioch Review,* XXIV (Summer 1964), 201–211.
    Chapter 3   ("The Closed Frontier and American Tragedy") from *The Texas Quarterly,* XI (Spring 1968), 56–69.
    Chapter 4   (*"Huckleberry Finn* as Tragedy") from *The Yale Review,* LIX (Summer 1970), 532–548.

To Les Elliott

Preface

At various stages in writing this book I have had helpful conversations with many friends, colleagues, and students. To try to acknowledge each of them by name would inevitably result in inadvertent omissions. However, to George N. Crosland and Philip E. Hager I am particularly indebted. The many occasions the three of us traveled the freeway, each to work on his own research, established what must be a permanent friendship. I am also indebted to Paul M. Reigstad who made his study on Ole Rölvaag available to me, and to Harrison Hayford who years ago showed me Melville's blank wall. I would be remiss if I failed to mention my wife and three children, who, in their inimitable ways, gave me the soul stuff to see this study through.

Grateful acknowledgment is also made to the following periodicals where certain sections of this book first appeared: *The Antioch Review, The Texas Quarterly,* and *The Yale Review.*

Seattle, Washington   H.P.S.
August 1970

Contents

The Closed Frontier

Studies in American Literary Tragedy

I

1

Prospects
and Limitations

I

For all the controversy raised by Frederick Jackson Turner's frontier thesis, no student of American civilization
would deny that the Western frontier influenced the character of this nation. Turner said the frontier was *the* most
important single influence. Other historians have argued
that capitalism, Puritanism, North and South sectionalism,
or the Constitution contributed more significantly to shaping the national character. Substantial claims support each
of these positions. Nevertheless, the frontier made America
an open society from the beginning. Because individuals
could move west—because they had a west to which they
could move—social mobility became one of America's dis-

3

tinguishing characteristics. Furthermore, mobility nurtured optimism. In the American consciousness the West symbolized hope; the West figured into the *process* of civilization, so that the process itself came to mean progress. From this point logic designated the West as synonymous with the American Dream.

Something primal was at work. Once again the old struggle between man and nature took on an immediacy unlike anything Europe had known for centuries. In America this titanic work engaged not only isolated adventurers but a whole society. This fact was manifest from the day colonists first stepped onto the new land. Nature was both friend and foe, and to forget this fact was to place in jeopardy not only physical survival but the human spirit. The struggle, like Prometheus's, challenged the American's resourcefulness and summoned his pride. Like Prometheus, he became a conqueror of nature, a great rebel whose independence was no less sacrosanct than his individualism. He also thought of himself as an Adam, one who merged with nature or, intuiting its mysterious power, achieved his own full measure through nature. Only as his spirit freed itself from the bondage of social institutions and became part and parcel of nature could he realize this fulfillment. The West, therefore, held the paradox that the American discovered as fundamental to his experience. To conquer nature or, in a mystical sense, to fuse with it; to appropriate it for the progress of civilization or, instead, to conform to its ineffable laws for the sake of true selfhood; to emulate an Andrew Carnegie or to follow a Henry David Thoreau—this was the American's choice as he faced west.

Whatever else the frontier contributed to American development, it gave people a great myth. As participants in this myth they felt that its colossal meaning ranged from personal and national destiny to human destiny itself. The myth proclaimed that on the open frontier a person could be reborn; he could have a second chance. Freed from the heavy accretions of culture, the frontiersman again could experience the pristine harmony between himself and nature; or, to prove his superiority, he again could battle nature's inscrutable ways and, through strength and resourcefulness, triumph over them. This same confidence imbuing the national spirit supported relentless expansionism and assured purity of motive. By the end of the nineteenth century the frontier was inseparable from national and international history. As both personal and social process, it clearly had become a phase in human experience. As myth it had confirmed political democracy, human infinitude, and philosophical idealism.

What then is the significance of the closed frontier in American history? This is a question Turner opened in his famous essay of 1893 but did not answer. He saw his task to be that of establishing the frontier's significance during the nineteenth century, not of exploring the ramifications of his fateful announcement that now, in the century's final decade, the frontier was closed. Others knew better than he what the real significance of this fact was. Mark Twain and Henry Adams knew what it was. So, later, did Ole Rölvaag and Nathanael West. Each in his way knew that the significance of the closed frontier was tragedy. The term was not restricted to a literary mode. Tragedy also meant a way of looking at life—at American life. This kind of tragedy touches the national psyche; it affects a people's collective consciousness and, perhaps, its unconscious as well. That the closed frontier served as the metaphor for American tragedy suggests that this tragedy, when accepted, destroyed illusions fostered on the open frontier and impelled the nation to come of age.

When a nation, like a person, comes of age, it recognizes that limitation is a fundamental fact of life. Painfully it admits that possibilities can only be finite and progress only limited, that solutions to problems are found more often through compromises than crusades. It discards illusions about national invincibility or the divine right to exercise power. It also abandons the dream that a second chance mollifies responsibilities here and now. Coming of age means awakening to the tragic realities that nations, like men, are only mortal; that truth comes chiefly through ambiguity and paradox; and that the old inheritance of pride still carries its inexorable consequences. These realities emphasize the common bondage all men share and the futility of their efforts to escape it. All this is the human condition, made tragic by the fact that pride and certain illusions live on. In our "universal bondage," says T. S. Eliot, we pretend "to be the uncommon exception."[1] To come of age is to recognize no exceptions, no annulments, and, most importantly, no escape from the cycle of genesis and decay. The existentialism symbolized by a closed frontier replaces the idealism engendered on an open frontier. Instead of a limitless frontier there is a wall. The tension comes from the illusory prospect of the one and the certitude of the other. Existence in this tension is the heart of tragedy.

II

In the past the term "frontier" clearly designated more than the western boundary of American settlement, more too than the seemingly endless free land beyond that line. As metaphor the term carried social, psychological, and philosophical meanings especially analogous to the American nineteenth-century spirit. Of particular importance is the way the metaphor of the open frontier served the Transcendentalists who preached the limitless potential of the human spirit. But of equal importance is the fact that other writers considered transcendence and reconciliation inconsistent with what Emerson himself called the "lords of life." The point to notice is that Turner's announcement in 1893 that the frontier was closed did not mark the beginnings of American tragedy, but it did corroborate, as it were, the closed wall as a metaphor accounting for the American's tragic limitations.

Emerson serves as an important figure illustrating how this metaphor supported philosophic speculation. As a kind of five-year distillation of his thought, Emerson wrote in his essay "Circles" that the life of man is like "a self-evolving circle," rushing always outward "to new and larger circles, and that without end." If the soul is "quick and strong," it "bursts" over the boundary on all sides, expanding ever farther. The heart, he says, "refuses to be imprisoned"; for it, there is no "outside, no inclosing wall, no circumference." The death of his son Waldo in 1842, however, severely shook Emerson's faith; and soon afterward he found himself struggling between the ideas of freedom and fate, between the open possibilities in one's merging with the All ("the currents of the Universal Being circulate through me") and the "immovable limitations" imposed by the lords of life.

In what according to Stephen A. Whicher is "probably his strongest essay,"[2] Emerson wrote the following year in "Experience" that these limitations—Illusion, Temperament, Succession, Surface, Surprise, Reality, Subjectiveness —were "in my way," but with new-found readiness he announced his acceptance of their "clangor and jangle." The easy synthesis in "Nature" and "The American Scholar" is not what he now depicts. Instead there is a growing awareness that experience belies reconciliation, and that wisdom consists in one's living within what Emerson calls "the middle region," "the temperate zone," "the mid-world," where in fact the limitations upon the human spirit find their analogy in a closed frontier. It must be noted that Emerson, not ready to accept a tragic view of life, manifests far less torment in his facing the wall than did Melville. In fact Emerson calls these limitations "beautiful," and then, in what seems more contradiction and paradox, he announces in this same essay that indeed "we have not arrived at a wall." He still envisions the time when he might "die out of nature," transcend the not-Me, and "be born again into this new yet unapproachable America I have found in the West."

One might suppose that Emerson's expansive design for experiencing universality of spirit would be more strenuously challenged in his later essay "The Tragic" (1844), but again the walls of limitation—famine, fever, inaptitude, mutilation, the rack, madness, the loss of friends—do not constitute final truth. They create terror and fear only among "imperfect characters." These contingencies are only superficial, just as tragedy is only illusory, belonging to life's exterior. He argues that pain enhances moral purity, so that instead of terror we come to know "tuneful tragedy," a condition, Emerson says, "whereinto these passionate clouds of sorrow cannot rise."

Even though Emerson begins this essay with the notable statement "He has seen but half the universe who never has been shown the House of Pain," it is clear that he never intended to limit truth to what lies this side of the wall. For all his skepticism, voiced again in his essay on Montaigne ("The astonishment of life is the absence of any appearance of reconciliation between the theory and practice of life"), Emerson's view extends beyond tragedy, beyond the boundaries of evil and fate. Evil, he insists, is merely the absence of good; or, stated positively, evil is good in the making, just as fate is human power that shall be. Fate refines and strengthens human will. "We stand against Fate," Emerson declares in his essay "Fate," "as children stand up against the wall in their father's house and notch their height from year to year." Giving fate its due, Emerson then transforms it into the means of man's own triumph: "calamities, oppositions, and weights are wings and means,—we are reconciled." Emerson would have us build altars to beautiful fate and believe that fate is nothing more than an illusory closed frontier that thought will someday master.

For Melville the circumscribing wall represents inexorable limitation. For one to try to remove the wall, to pretend it does not exist, or to strike through it is as tragically tempting as it is fatal. Edwin Fussell points out that to Melville the image of the frontier rarely suggested peace and mediation, let alone transcendence, but rather chaos and horror. After the closing of the frontier, which Fussell marks as concurrent with the Civil War, Melville found himself more desperate than ever, writing *The Confidence-Man* as a testimony, says Fussell, of a time when "all the values the national culture had been optimistically attributing to the Western frontier were suddenly inverted, and harmony and reconciliation were revealed to be chaos and nightmare." Instead of a trail of truth, the West represented to Melville "a trail of error, a continental mistake, the way to insanity."[3] To support this judgment Fussell refers to Melville's statement in *Pierre* (Chapter 9) that in seeking truth too far man "loses the directing compass of his mind"; and as if arriving at the Pole he finds that the needle "indifferently respects all points of the horizon alike." The frontier becomes a chartless metaphysical emptiness. But to Melville the frontier also suggests a boundary, an imprisoning wall, and the task of trying to penetrate it is no less than the way to insanity.

Ominous shadowings of this image occur in Melville's early fiction, even though they do not directly relate to the American frontier as such. In *Mardi* he caught the ambiguity of what he called the "boundless boundary of the West," but in *Redburn* and *White Jacket* the image merely suggests confinement and oppression. The narrator Redburn speaks of being "hemmed in" by the darkness of night, as if the black night on the ocean were a great gulf with "beetling black cliffs" all around. A more intense feeling of confinement presses upon the sailor White Jacket, subjected to the martial law of the Navy from which "there is no escape" and figuratively restricted by his jacket, "white as a shroud," its "masoned-up pockets" weighted with all manner of accumulation. Only as the narrative ends does he burst from his jacket, which had stuck on him "like the fatal shirt of Nessus," and to what extent he is free depends upon the inscrutable ways of the "coiled fish," a white shark, which brushes by him at that same moment.

The wall with its related images is central in *Moby-Dick.* Melville repeatedly depicts characters who, for all their dignity and democratic worth, confront a superior force or an object embodying power, mystery, or injustice. Like Ahab, the prisoner may have the grandeur of a demigod, yet is inferior in this confrontation. In prolific images, unmistakable as they accrue, Melville presents the inferior as one who suffers a grievance or woe, one who is physically wounded, mutilated, dismembered—or immobile, frozen, paralyzed, compressed. What he faces may be a wall, mountain, pyramid, inscription, tattoo, hieroglyphic, scroll, tombstone, picture—typically suggestive of some problem, riddle, secret. He may confront the Sperm Whale's head, finding it a "dead, blind wall," an "impregnable, uninjurable wall." Or he may fight against fierce winds, wear an "iron crown," uphold "on his frozen brow the piled entablatures of ages," resemble a "captive king," live "enveloped in whale-lines," and typify the condition that all men share— "born with halters round their necks." Like Ishmael, he asks, "Who aint a slave?"; like Ahab, living in "the masoned, walled-town of a Captain's exclusiveness," he voices his plight: "I feel deadly faint, bowed, and humped, as though I were Adam, staggering beneath the piled centuries since Paradise." And, like Tashtego atop the main-truck, he inevitably goes down, the final image that of a "captive form" folded in Ahab's flag (the Stars and Stripes?).

In Melville's subsequent work this image remains all-important for his tragic view of man. Resolved to rescue Isabel, Pierre leaves Saddle Meadows and his ancestral house, which at once seemed to have "contracted to a nut-shell around him; the walls smote his forehead." The obstacles he overcomes only provide the prelude to the tragic fact that in the end "ambiguities . . . hemmed him in; the stony walls [were] all round that he could not overleap." Using the same image Melville describes Israel Potter, quickened by this tragic vision, as one to whom "the sense of being masoned up in the wall, grew, and grew, and grew upon him." Slaves and fetters in "Benito Cereno" provide the same oppressive theme that walls suggest in "Bartleby the Scrivener." Outside the lawyer's window was the omnipresent "lofty brick wall, black by age and everlasting shade." Bartleby's window commanded "no view at all," his fate unchanged in the Tombs where the narrator sees Bartleby for the last time, "his face towards a high wall." A sense of "penal hopelessness" pervades "The Encantadas," and the wisdom Billy Budd and his fellow sailors learn on board the *Bellipotent* is that "forms, measured forms are everything."

Of the ambivalent possibilities for action when his characters confront the pasteboard mask, the blank wall, the closed frontier, Melville most frequently dramatizes two: aggression and quiescence. Illustrative of the first is a movement, often sudden and violent, against the superior force or object. The aim is to destroy it, to strike through it, to penetrate or uncover its mystery. But aggression fails; the blow rebounds and causes self-destruction. Quiescence, on the other hand, is enacted through some variety of endurance, resignation, submission, or withdrawal. It allows various conditions of survival, few happy, with any increase of happiness paid for by the loss of independence and dignity.

Confrontation may therefore lead, at one extreme, to Ahab's final action and words: ". . . to the last I grapple with thee; from hell's heart I stab at thee; for hate's sake I spit my last breath at thee." Or it may show us a Bartleby, whose doleful refrain—"I prefer not to"—represents the other extreme.

Where in the range of possible action Melville sighted his own direction is less important than where he envisioned the common democratic man's position to be, the man whom Melville describes in Chapter 26 of *Moby-Dick*. This man is clearly the Westerner whose abounding dignity shines "in the arm that wields a pick or drives a spike"; or he is the common sailor, even the renegade. Unlike Ahab and Bartleby, this man radiates the spirit of equality and is, in short, man "in the ideal." In characteristic imagery Melville describes this man as one who shares with everyone the "universal thump," the pain and catastrophe and always the limitations imposed by his human condition. Whether seen from "a physical or metaphysical point of view," this condition promises no reprieve or transcendence, only at best the earthly dignity that comes from indefinite endurance and endless striving. In one of Melville's great descriptions of tragic beingness, he recalls in "The Encantadas" a night when, lying on his bunk, he listened to the "draggings and concussions" of a giant tortoise on the belittered deck overhead. "At sunrise I found him butted like a battering-ram against the immovable foot of the foremast, and still striving, tooth and nail, to force the impossible passage." Musing about tortoises, Melville continues: "I have known them in their journeyings ram themselves heroically against rocks, and long abide there, nudging, wriggling, wedging, in order to displace them, and so hold on their inflexible path."

For all Melville's disenchantment with the nation's westward movement—which, according to Fussell, Melville finally came to regard with "a sense of total irrelevance"[4] —the more important point is that he denied the teleological West. For him the closed wall depicted the world men live in. Human finitude dooms their heroic effort to force passage through the wall and to gain universal Oneness.

Like Melville, Emily Dickinson augured what Turner was later to announce as historic fact. Her spiritual explorations reached distances as great as those Melville traveled, and her metaphysical sense of the closed frontier was just as certain. Overshadowing her faith in Christian transcendence was the constant certainty: "I'm finite—I cant see." In her poem "Their Hight in Heaven comforts not," she finds little security in either the "House of Supposition" (the Church and its tenuous doctrines) or the "Glimmering Frontier" that "Skirts the Acres of Perhaps." Speculation about "moments of Escape" in her poem "The Soul has Bandaged moments" suddenly suggests delirious freedom. The long-dungeoned soul, "bursting all the doors," dances abroad and almost touches paradise, only to be "retaken" by the "Felon," then shackled and stapled. Personifying dark mortality, the Felon proves his sovereignty no less than Melville's "feline Fate."

Throughout nineteenth- and twentieth-century American literature the metaphor of the closed frontier and its related images serves this tragic theme. One thinks of Gilbert Osmond's four walls wherein Isabel comes of age; or Jay Gatsby's futile reaching for the green light; or Jake Barnes's cyclic wanderings that take him back to where he started, back to Madrid where "all the trains finish. . . . They don't go on anywhere"; or the voices George Willard hears whispering "a message concerning the limitations of life." One thinks also of Joe Christmas:

> Looking, he can see the smoke low on the sky, beyond an imperceptible corner; he is entering it again, the

> street which ran for thirty years. It had been a paved
> street, where going should be fast. It had made a circle
> and he is still inside of it. Though during the last seven
> days he has had no paved street, yet he has travelled
> farther than in all the thirty years before. And yet he
> is still inside the circle. "And yet I have been farther
> in these seven days than in all the thirty years," he
> thinks. "But I have never got outside that circle. I have
> never broken out of the ring of what I have already
> done and cannot ever undo," he thinks quietly.

Something undeniably American gives this account its
strange power. That the striving to get away only brings one
back to himself is the irony of American exploration,
whether geographic or spiritual. Something similarly
American is in the names—Jack Burden and Jim Burden—
which Robert Penn Warren and Willa Cather give to their
respective narrators. Perhaps the American is J. B., whose
Old Testament counterpart knew what it was like to be
"hedged in." That the frontier promised freedom from the
burden of history was the great American Dream. Nothing
less than the tragic vision could shatter it.

III

The three writers chosen to illustrate the tragedy inherent in the closed frontier—Mark Twain, Ole Rölvaag, and
Nathanael West—are not usually associated with the frontier as such. More specifically, Twain's *The Adventures of
Huckleberry Finn* and *A Connecticut Yankee in King Arthur's Court*—two of his books to be discussed at length—
do not utilize the American frontier setting, unless one considers as frontier the territory Huck intends "to light out"
to at the end of the novel. The two books nevertheless present what might be called frontier assumptions that go to

the center of American tragedy. With the prison as the key image in *Huckleberry Finn* Twain dramatized the conflict between bondage and freedom. The ironic resolution shows that Huck and Jim, both imprisoned in one way or another, are free; whereas Tom, who enjoys freedom from social contumely, is actually a prisoner of that same society. The freedom Huck and Jim know, if only briefly, comes because of their common bondage. Recognizing this condition frees them to love as persons, yet knowing that their society tolerates no such love. The metaphor of a closed frontier shows them thrust together, each depending upon the other's humanity. Theirs is an I-Thou humanity, a far different kind from the self-sufficiency that frontierism fostered. Their humanity enfolds weakness and guilt, suffering and self-denial, and for this reason it is tragic. This is the humanity that society, founded upon optimistic assumptions, can never tolerate.

Although Ole Rölvaag's trilogy depicts early life on the Dakota prairies, only the first novel captures their awesome magnitude—and this to show the Norwegian immigrants not as conquerors but as lonely exiles conquered by the frontier. Like Twain in *Huckleberry Finn,* Rölvaag was concerned with what happens to people whose frontier offered no escape from personal and cultural entanglements. The metaphor of the closed frontier again serves, this time to suggest the cleavage between cultures and generations, between the Old World and the New, between superficial adaptation and hidden estrangement. Rölvaag's great theme is the cost of immigration, and in his three novels this cost is visited successively upon Per Hansa, his wife, Beret, and their son, Peder. Rölvaag's decision to portray this family as players in a vast tragedy—one in which an open frontier proved only illusory—struck at what finally may be the essence of the frontier experience. A people had crossed the Atlantic in search of a new Garden of Eden, only to discover that freedom was a delusion and a curse. Again like Twain, Rölvaag questioned the assumption that time and place can create something entirely new. Both writers sent their characters in search of new beginnings, but the truth to be discovered was that all that this time and this place can provide is the inevitable tragedy of broken illusions and human contingencies.

It is with Nathanael West that American tragedy becomes something surrealistic and nightmarish. The westward trek of Americans, growing pathological in their optimism, finally ends in southern California, a region inhabited by the totally deluded. Nothing is real. Life is as make-believe as Hollywood movie sets where make-believe heroes eat cardboard sandwiches in front of cellophane waterfalls. West's first three novels portend the Dantesque world of the fourth, *The Day of the Locust,* in which the mythical journey westward proves to be the tragedy of the closed frontier. Iowa folk have arrived at their Promised Land, their Golden Gate, and finding only California at their feet they desperately design their architecture to resemble the dream world that first sent them west. They design their lives the same way. But the existential panic following their boredom and then their discovery that the American Dream is a cheat sends them into mass violence, as if violence alone can satisfy their craving for the fulfillment the frontier promised but never supplied. Violence in West's fiction is not romantic primitivism. It has nothing to do with the kind of natural or even cosmic violence found in Ahab's world. In Hollywood nature is as dead as Fitzgerald's Valley of Ashes or Eliot's Waste Land. Violence in *The Day of the Locust* is human self-destruction, like the violence of Hiroshima, which in the final pages of his book *Errand into the Wilderness,* Perry Miller finds as that errand's apocalyptic ending.

To conclude a study about tragedy in the mythical

West is, almost fatefully, to consider eschatology. What is the American way of death? Jessica Mitford wryly suggests that American funeral directors have satisfied themselves with answers. Their cosmetics have conquered death, and Hollywood's Forest Lawn has transformed it into the best of all possible worlds. That euphemism and deceit permeate the American way of both life and death is exactly Nathanael West's theme, for in neither is tragedy allowed. In West's last novel, violence is the antidote for a people's somnambulism. Nothing short of total conflagration will awaken the masses to the fact that death is the wall against which life is performed. Fervently West's Tod Hackett paints "The Burning of Los Angeles," his own shock of recognition. But the greater shock comes when West unites the art with the reality. Truth is destruction; destruction, truth. The overwhelming irony is that destruction is the truth of the frontier dream. This is Nathanael West's eschatological vision, one that both Mark Twain and Henry Adams shared half a century earlier. *A Connecticut Yankee in King Arthur's Court* and *The Education of Henry Adams* are works of eschatology. They contain more than a mere longing for the past, so unmistakable, for example, in Hemingway's *Green Hills of Africa*. These two books squarely confront the last things, and it is small matter whether the end comes in violence or entropy.

To incorporate eschatology into an American frontier heritage promising rebirth is like spanning the antipodes. Yet the ultimate paradox of tragedy requires this total view. As the hard lines of an etching stand out only against blankness, so tragedy shows human acts to be meaningful only when they contrast with the nothingness of death. To soften the background is to reduce the intensity of the line; to pretend no background exists is to lose the line completely. Only against a closed frontier can one's actions and dreams take on configuration, perhaps even beauty.

2

Frederick Jackson Turner: Frontier History as Symbol

I

The Wisconsin historian Frederick Jackson Turner was not the first American to call attention to the frontier. The frontier idea in America goes back to the early seventeenth-century journals of William Byrd, William Bradford, and John Winthrop, back to the time when America's frontier was the lush Carolina hills and the rock-bound New England coast. It goes back to Hector St. Jean de Crèvecoeur, whose *Letters from an American Farmer,* published in 1793, announced that on the American frontier "individuals of all nations are melted into a new race of men"; or back to less enthusiastic observers who, like Timothy Dwight of Yale, associated the frontier with unlettered bumpkins. Regardless of viewpoint, Americans acknowledged a frontier early in their history. Thomas Jefferson expanded it with the Louisiana Purchase; Andrew Jackson, our first log-cabin president, represented it in the White House; Abraham Lincoln drew his ideals from it; and John F. Kennedy hailed it anew.

But Frederick Jackson Turner, born in Portage, Wisconsin, in 1862, was the first American historian to say outright that the frontier *explained* America. To Turner the fundamental fact in the nation's history was the "ever retreating frontier of free land." This fact, he said, was "the key to American development." People from many different countries came together at the frontier, where they blended into an American "composite nationality." This frontier experience distinguished Americans from all other people of the world, said Turner, for it gave them an identity separate from Old World traditions. It developed a jealously guarded individualism and laid the groundwork for democracy. On this point Turner was adamant. Democracy, he said, was not imported into Virginia on the *Sarah Constant* or into Plymouth on the *Mayflower* but was born in "the American forest."[1]

Since it was first dramatically announced in 1893, the Turner thesis has been the subject of much controversy. His defenders have amplified the thesis, and many historians today still think it sound. Others feel that Turner was guilty of dangerous oversimplifications, while there are still others who see Turner's main contribution to be not his frontier hypothesis at all but rather his concept of physiographic "sections." The smoke has not yet cleared, nor is it likely it ever will. The controversy only calls attention to Turner's posture. Every student of American civilization at one time or another confronts the Turner thesis. Professor Benjamin W. F. Wright, Jr., who questioned many of Turner's assumptions, called him "the most brilliant and most influential of

American historians."[2] More recently Professor Merle
Curti has said that in "originality" and "influence" Frederick Jackson Turner "has thus far had no superior if he has
had any peer."[3] The consensus now seems to be that Turner
ranks with Francis Parkman as one of America's two greatest historians of their native ground.

It is not enough to say that Turner's fame rests upon
his frontier hypothesis without also pointing out the great
importance his literary style gave the work. Among the
relatively few historians who have actually paid attention
to Turner's literary art, none has regarded it as integral to
the hypothesis itself. One of Turner's severest critics, John
C. Almack, blamed Turner's "unusually happy phrasing"
and "charming style" for the fact that readers, deceived by
his style, were unwisely led to believe his doctrine.[4] Professor Wright acknowledged his "grand manner"; but, said
Wright, Turner's poetic capacity to write "brilliant and
moving odes to the glories of the westward movement" was
"more misleading than it [was] helpful."[5] A. O. Craven
praised Turner as a "careful, scholarly craftsman in spite of
the fact that he undoubtedly viewed history as an art rather
than as a science."[6] Even Henry Nash Smith, both a literary
scholar and a historian, is uneasy in following Turner from
a plane of abstraction to one of metaphor and myth, by
which process Turner transformed the American forest into
an enchanted wood and the frontiersman into a reborn
American. What especially disturbed Professor Smith was
that Turner's metaphors threatened "to become themselves
a means of cognition and to supplement discursive reason-
ing."[7]

The obvious fact is that historians distrust poetic language on the grounds that in some way it alters and even
invalidates scientific findings. That Turner's hypothesis was
couched in language supposedly restricted only to the
imaginative poet unsettled many of his own colleagues

while, paradoxically, compelling them to return again and again to his words. His essays are in fact what the English romantic Thomas DeQuincy would have called "literature of power." Brilliant imagery, poetic cadences, plus metaphor that becomes epical in its proportions give to his frontier hypothesis a vitality and penumbra of symbolic importance integral to the hypothesis itself.

It is not irrelevant to recall Aristotle's distinction between poetry and history. In the *Poetics* he argued that poetry is nobler than history because the poet is more philosophic, more serious than the historian and because he represents the ideal—what ought to be—not merely the historical or factual truth. In much the same way Dr. Johnson in eighteenth-century England ranked poetry well above history on the grounds that imagination, for the historian, "is not required in any high degree." Just how close historians have come to the level of poetic art is readily seen in Thucydides, Herodotus, Gibbon, Macaulay, and Carlyle. No one would deny these writers supreme literary distinction.

What has happened since the turn of the century is indicated by Karl Shapiro's query: "What was the dark day in time when History, one of the greatest of literary arts, put its tail between its legs and called itself a scientific puppy dog?"[8] What has happened, of course, is that history has become a social science. Deeply disturbed by the historian's decline and fall from his place among the humanities, Arthur M. Schlesinger, Jr., describes present-day historical writing as "dry, detailed, dusty investigations, deliberately devoid of sentiment, of comment, and of grace."[9]

This is not the place to argue history's kinship with either social science or the humanities. Turner conceived his task as historian to rest with both. Nothing would deter him from the painstaking discipline required of a historical researcher. Carl Becker, one of his early students at the University of Wisconsin, vividly remembered Turner coming to class, his immense brief case bulging with the notes of a morning's labor in the library.[10] In Turner's office were to be found population studies, maps, charts of every kind and description, manila envelopes stuffed with notes, all testifying to Turner's insistence that documentary evidence was of unquestioned importance. Yet facts alone never wrote history, and Turner was a supreme writer. As he announced in his early essay "The Significance of History" (1891), the historian's responsibility is to discover the inexorable relationship of evidence. This task presupposes one's finding a continuity to history, an organic and ever-changing life behind the facts. To use facts without making theory was inexcusable to Turner. But Turner went a step further, and it was this step that took him into the realm of art, into what Professor Schlesinger has called the historian's "aesthetic vision." Through the welter of facts and theories Turner beheld American society not as an object for dry, technical analysis but rather as a viable organism whose essence could be described only symbolically. Turner's art is not merely those qualities of prose and language noted by some of his readers. It is also his consciousness of society as both unity and continuity and his imaginative power to find a symbol in which his vision coheres.

II

Turner's symbol is the frontier. It is of only minor importance that, taken literally, the frontier signified a "line" up to which population had reached the figure of at least two persons per square mile. Again on the literal level, it is not particularly significant that in 1893 Turner announced the disappearance of a statistical "frontier line." What is important is that in the symbol of the frontier Turner captured the emotions and visions of an entire nation.

Even as an undergraduate at the University of Wisconsin Turner leaned toward a poetic interpretation of history, or, more accurately, he read the poets as the best interpreters of their age. His university prize-winning essay, "The Poet of the Future," written in 1883 when he was a junior, is full of such imagery as the following:

> We open the lay of Beowulf, and as we read the poet's page, the walls grow unsubstantial and stretch away in the somber forests and rugged homes of the wild north land; we feel the salt gusts of the sea, the dampness of the wilderness is about us, and we hear the symphony of the wind among the pine trees. We are back again in the fierce, rude youth of our race, of which these songs are poetic crystallizations.

This description suggests a key quality of Turner's mind, namely, the desire to capture the feeling as well as the fact, to return imaginatively to "the fierce, rude youth of our race" in order to understand the vitalism of the present. At Wisconsin young Turner was caught up in Emersonianism and, like the Concord philosopher, declared that man can rediscover the world's foundations, filled, he said, "with life, with meaning, with dignity." Democracy, he said, "is waiting for its poet" who will sing "the divinity of man and nature."[11]

What this lofty idealism meant for himself, an outsetting historian, Turner was not long in announcing. In "The Significance of History"—the first of his great essays written after he joined the University of Wisconsin faculty in 1891 —he set virtually no limits to his task and duty. Nothing less than the "self-consciousness of humanity" was to be his high calling, and in this calling he would summon not only the invocation of the Church *Sursum corda* ("lift up your hearts") but all the "interpretative power" a historian can bring to his work. Turner never repudiated this aim, nor did he ever lose the poetic vision that for him was best exemplified in the high-ringing poetry of James Russell Lowell, Kipling, Emerson, Whitman, and Tennyson. Throughout his career the feature Turner found common to these poets was faith in a new order of things, in the democratic ideal, which for the Wisconsin historian meant, above all, faith in the American Dream. "Let us dream as our fathers dreamt," he wrote in his essay "The West and American Ideals" (1914), "and let us make our dreams come true." This dream for Turner was like that of Tennyson's Ulysses —"To strive, to seek, to find and not to yield." Such was Turner's unflagging idealism, even though a new century was bringing in social, economic, and political upheaval that left such optimism high and dry, and that, at the same time, ushered in a new generation of historians sharply critical of Turner's idealization of the American frontier.

Yet students of American history have continued to read Turner. They recognize that Turner attempted to depict the frontier as an epic, serving to unify not only the American saga but man's total history, past and present. At the same time a few readers specifically note that Turner followed the procedure of poetry that, said Professor Smith in writing about Turner, is "to imagine an ideal so vividly that it comes to seem actual,"[12] another way of saying that the *significance* of the frontier was born with Turner's esthetic vision of it.

In a remarkable way Turner resembles Thoreau, who proceeded to choose Walden Pond and its surrounding hills as the place where he would "mine." Turner chose the frontier, "a fertile field for investigation," he said. Like Thoreau, Turner discovered his rich ore to be the existence of vital forces lying beneath nature and civilization, and calling them both into life. Metaphysically, Thoreau mined more deeply, yet both he and Turner arrived at essentially the same conclusion about past and present history: history is unified and continuous, and the most fitting image describing it is that of an organism. As Turner explained in "Problems in American History" (1892), the frontier maps he studied in *Scribner's Statistical Atlas* revealed clues to a frontier dynamism. "Perceive," he said, "that the dark portion flows forward like water on an uneven surface; here and there are tongues of settlement pushed out in advance, and corresponding projections of wilderness wedged into the advancing mass." Here was the frontier made synonymous with movement, expansion, evolution. Here on the frontier was to be seen "the steady growth of a complex nervous system for the originally simple inert continent." Out of what Turner called "inert" nature grew a society, a nation, a civilization, all of it a mighty drama unfolding from east to west.

What he saw being enacted on the frontier was the *process* of civilization—of a people transforming the elemental into the complex, the wild into the cultured, the primitive into the civilized. To Turner the American frontier story recapitulated the story of man's total history. His monumental essay entitled "The Significance of the Frontier in American History" (1893) is a powerful work of the imagination, imposing order and meaning on anarchic experience. As Professor Craven observed, Turner "lifted the story of simple, scattered localities, engaged in the homely tasks of living and living better, into the dignity of world history."[13] Something far more than a national story is behind Turner's often quoted sentence: "Stand at Cumberland Gap and watch the procession of civilization, marching single file—the buffalo following the trail to salt springs, the

Indian, the fur trader and hunter, the cattle raiser, the pioneer farmer." Nothing less than the myth of man's conquest of nature is the meaning of his symbolic frontier.

In this essay, terms such as the pioneer's "dominion over nature," his "progress from savage conditions," and his evolution "into a higher state" strongly suggest what was the heart of Turner's frontier thesis. Even though Turner argued, too loosely, that the frontier united heterogeneous peoples into a "composite nationality," and that it served to free the new American from his European past, the real point of both his esthetic and moral vision was the Promethean struggle of man to overcome his subservience to nature and its dark gods. Though for Turner the outcome was never in doubt, the struggle itself first saw the wilderness master the colonist, who, to survive at all, had to put on the hunting shirt and the moccasin, plant Indian corn and plow with a sharp stick, shout the "war cry" and take "the scalp in orthodox Indian fashion." But "little by little" the tide of battle favored the civilized white man—the ambassador of reason, enlightenment, and progress. This essay of 1893 presents that titanic struggle as the ultimately significant fact in American history. From this conclusion it becomes clear that subduing nature or transforming it to serve his own purposes describes the American's manifest destiny.

Turner was not yet done with symbol in this essay, the most enigmatical of all being his use of the term "rebirth." Each time the westward-moving American advanced on the frontier, his return to primitive conditions or his encounter with savagery led to a "perennial rebirth." The entire sentence is worth quoting: "This perennial rebirth, this fluidity of American life, this expansion westward with its new opportunities, its continuous touch with the simplicity of primitive society, furnish the forces dominating American character." To interpret Turner's rebirth symbol is to strike hard upon the other key word in the sentence—"opportunities." First stripped of his cultural accumulations, the settler then becomes uniquely self-reliant by developing "stalwart and rugged qualities." This experience is a kind of Thoreauvian "moulting season," an opportunity for the frontiersman to renew his energies, inventiveness, self-confidence, and optimism. Like America's other great nineteenth-century romantics, Turner vaguely felt some occult power in nature that liberated a man from pettiness and allowed him to grow to his full measure. Yet paradoxically it was this same full measure that impelled him to dominate nature. At this point Turner parts company with America's romantic poets, including Thoreau. The new-born man in Thoreau's conception is one who, through a process of simplifying, drives life into a corner, reduces it to its basic terms, and discovers therein a spiritual reality akin to his own essence. Thoreau's ritual of rebirth awakened man to the ineluctable mystery of life and to his own participation in it. Walt Whitman's ritual transformed man into a new personality, fresh in the knowledge not only that he was participating in a cosmic design but also that he was the agent shaping it, fulfilling it. No such metaphysical ramifications grow out of Turner's frontier ritual. Instead of mystically realizing selfhood by losing it in the spirit of nature ("I am nothing; I become all," said Emerson), Turner's reborn Westerner is essentially rechallenged—to strive, to seek, to find and *not to yield*. The challenge is not to simplify but to organize, to utilize—or, to use the word most relevant, to civilize. A new personality does appear but it is not the one Whitman describes in "Song of Myself." It is the Captain of Industry, in Turner's view the flower of Western civilization.

It would be a mistake to link Turner with the Social

Darwinists, whose view of life contained far more jungle than frontier ethics. Turner insisted that though rude and gross the frontiersman was not a materialist. "This early Western man was an idealist" who endlessly "dreamed dreams and beheld visions." Turner stated in "Contributions of the West to American Democracy" (1903) that it would be wrong "to write of the West as though it were engrossed in mere material ends." More important, he thought, was the fact that the West fostered ideals of individualism, competitiveness, and democratic self-government. Practiced by such Western leaders as George Rogers Clark, Abraham Lincoln, Andrew Jackson, and William Henry Harrison, these ideals Turner presently saw exemplified in John D. Rockefeller, Marcus Hanna, Claus Spreckels, Marshall Field, and Andrew Carnegie. Something of the Westerner Turner found in each: Rockefeller, a son of a New York farmer; Hanna, still a Cleveland grocery clerk at twenty; Field, a farm boy in Massachusetts; and Carnegie, a ten-year-old emigrant from Scotland. Hailing them as "the great geniuses that have built up the modern industrial concentration," Turner was especially struck by the fact that they were trained "in the midst of democratic society." Their ideals were identical to those of the pioneer in his log cabin.

Of course Turner's successors enjoyed a heyday in attacking this brand of democratic idealism. They saw nothing more in America's so-called forest philosophy than rapacious claim-holders employing any means to get rich quicker. Questions dealing with race and class exploitation, suffrage, unions, overseas imperialism, reforms, and countless other issues delineating the new century, these critics accused Turner of ignoring. A year after Turner's death, Louis M. Hacker in *The Nation* went so far as to say that another generation of historical scholars will be needed to correct Turner's ideas, which, Hacker asserted, were not only "fictitious" but "positively harmful."[14]

III

After all the debate, what remains of Turner's frontier hypothesis? No one has yet successfully refuted the fact that the frontier was significant in American development. Moreover, the image of the frontiersman is one that Americans to this day still cherish. But of equal significance is the historian himself, the man whose imagination gave final shape and vitality to the theory and whose imagery brought it to the level of art.

Often overlooked in assessments of Turner is his private agony, much like Henry Adam's, in seeing the American Dream change into something more violent than he had earlier envisioned. It must be remembered that in his important essay of 1893 describing the triumphant frontiersman, Turner also announced the momentous fact that the frontier was now closed. The reader can hardly miss the tension sustained throughout the essay between the dream and the fact—the dream that to the west would always be a frontier where man could confront the new and raw environment and master it; and the fact that this geographic and psychological safety valve was shut tight. Just as Henry Adams in the same year viewed America's future in the immense dynamos he saw exhibited at the Chicago World's Fair— dynamos symbolizing the multiplicity and disintegration of the oncoming century—so Turner in viewing a closed frontier wondered what America's destiny would be when free land was no longer available to allow a person opportunity to compete unrestrictedly for the resources of the land and when laissez-faire democracy was brought under the constraint of paternalistic government. The essay's opening announcement, taken from the Superintendent of the Census bulletin of 1890, that "there can hardly be said to be a frontier line," echoes throughout the essay and, in the final sentence, sounds once more, ominously: "And now, four centuries from the discovery of America, at the end of a hundred years of life under the Constitution, the frontier has gone, and with its going has closed the first period of American history."

Rather than amplifying what the next period would bring, Turner remained in the past and indefatigably sought to understand it. To him the dates and events of western expansion were dead facts until the lifeblood of the peoples of that era, their hopes, failures, fears, and triumphs, could bring meaning to the chronology of fact. Turner's writing reflects his own quest to feel and to know the cumulative experience of those Americans who headed west. He evoked the feeling of subtle forces underlying the external facts— dynamic activity, restless seeking, opposition and conflict, aggressiveness, domination; a sense of unseen forces in the wilderness, the raw and sleeping giants of trade, agrarianism, industrialization. The words he repeatedly used— "democracy," "frontier," "expansion," "civilization," "savagery"—have connotations that are themselves accretions of age-old myth and symbol. "Waves of emigrants," "the ever richer tide" of people pouring into the Middle West suggest the waters of the original sea spawning its living organisms upon the land's edge. Routes of America's great rivers become "arteries made by geology." The vestigial remains of each frontier are made analogous to the terminal remains of successive glaciations, and comparing one frontier line with another is like "tracing patiently the shores of ancient seas."

Clearly, Turner's imagination perceived in the American frontier a mythical quality that raised his account far above mere factual description. In *The Interpretation of History* Paul Tillich asserts that "all historical writing which is to be taken seriously must have in it this mythical element," which reaches back into "original epochs" and ahead to "final epochs."[15] This kind of writing demands of the historian an artist's mythical consciousness to interpret the materials at hand in symbolic terms autochthonous to the time, the group, and the individuals involved. For Americans this original epoch was the dream, its symbolic expression the frontier where the dream could be corroborated. Turner's life-long quest to interpret the symbol stopped short at this point in time where the symbol was dying. The psychological if not spiritual consequences to a people bereft of both this dream and this symbol signaled for Turner another epoch, perhaps as with Henry Adams a final one, which Turner chose not to explore. To those persons who have groped into the next epoch the symbol of the frontier has been replaced by the wall, with no exit, such as that wall confronted by Arthur Miller's Willy Loman, the American who existentially discovers the meaning of tragedy and, one might add, who would not be deceived by what today suddenly appears to be a new safety valve in outer space.

3

The Closed Frontier
and American Tragedy

I

Today's students of American history study Frederick
Jackson Turner's frontier hypothesis far more critically
than they did in the 1890s when the young University of
Wisconsin professor first presented it. We now think, for
example, that in explaining American development
primarily in terms of Western expansion Turner overlooked
such influential groups as Southern agrarians, Eastern capi-
talists, and Middle Western Progressives; and that in
homogenizing a complex American society into what he
called a "composite nationality" he stereotyped Americans
and gave much too important a role to the geographic and
climatic factors shaping their development. Furthermore,

his so-called safety-valve theory failed to consider that the Western homesteader, wishing for a chance to fulfill his dreams of independence, had to cope with such obstacles as unscrupulous land speculators and railroad monopolists. Other issues come to mind when one thinks about Turner's frontier theory. Was the growth of American democracy isolated from the rest of Western civilizaton? Turner asserted it was. "American democracy," he wrote in "The West and American Ideals," "came out of the American forest, and it gained new strength each time it touched a new frontier." No one had disposed of American intellectual history, rooted in European thought, faster than Turner did. And, finally, what did Turner mean by democracy? Did he mean egalitarianism or something closer akin to Social Darwinism whereby in unrestricted competition the strong become stronger? How did Turner's concept of democracy speak to such issues as woman suffrage or to race and class exploitation? To these questions Turner failed to give compelling answers.

One must be careful not to claim more from Turner than he deserves. His interpretation of American development is not the only one, though for at least three decades after it first appeared it was hailed as such.[1] It is legitimate to say that Turner's view was overly simplified. Nevertheless, he still stands as a major figure in American historiography. And the reason must be that he saw into something fundamentally true about this land and its people. As the nineteenth century came to an end, it was as if some spokesman once again, and perhaps for the final time, had to testify to the myth that had sustained America since its discovery.

In his essay "The Significance of the Frontier in American History" (1893) he had said: "The existence of an area of free land, its continuous recession, and the advance of American settlement westward, *explain* American development" [italics added]. Thus was born his famous frontier hypothesis. Turner then went on, using poetic imagery, to tell how the frontiersman advanced over a "simple, inert continent" and left behind, as evidence of progress and development, a "complex nervous system." Turner's central metaphor was that of an awakened organism, once inert but now, with the westward march of civilization, a uniquely American nervous system—alive, changing, growing, evolving. As for the frontiersman, his continual "return" to the primitive and elemental provided a "perennial rebirth." Like America's great romantics Thoreau and Whitman, Turner believed that nature liberated man from the confinement of his society. On the frontier he became a new man, freed from the past with all its tradition and involvement, to say nothing of its complexity, corruption, and prejudice.

Turner restated what American visionaries before him had dreamed about. The colonists had seen a profoundly Biblical significance in their work. As Perry Miller put it, their mission was an "errand into the wilderness," there to undergo punitive testing and to find providential reward.[2] They were the chosen people, their hope millennial, their land a "New English Canaan." To Thomas Morton New England's summer beauty made the land "seem paradise." Increase Mather thought it a Kingdom of Christ "restored to its Paradise state."[3] Towns bearing such names as Harmony, Concord, New Hope, and Zion clearly indicated the sense of destiny that the American, as a new Adam, felt. In studying this visionary spirit, H. Richard Niebuhr has cogently entitled his book *The Kingdom of God in America.*

By the nineteenth century Americans saw what R. W. B. Lewis calls "the apotheosis of Adam."[4] This was also the century of America's great westward expansion. While Emerson in Concord was saying that "our day of dependence, our long apprenticeship to the learning of other lands, draws to a close," Cooper's Natty Bumppo demonstrated to what epical proportions the frontiersman could grow. While

Thoreau was saying in *Walden* that the dawn of this new day will make our present sun as but a morning star, and while Whitman sang of himself as an ever-growing, ever-enlarging personality that "fillest the vastnesses of Space," out on the frontier the Daniel Boones and Davy Crocketts were acting upon this new faith. In his book *The Oregon Trail* Francis Parkman used the term "jumping off" to describe the pioneers' departure, many of them from that town in Missouri auspiciously called Independence.[5]

Jumping off meant keeping ahead of oppressive complexities. It meant separation from the past, new adventure, new history, new being. It meant the American Dream, a virgin land, a golden gate, an open road. In short, it meant Eden. "The Edenic myth," writes Charles L. Sanford in *The Quest for Paradise,* "has been the most powerful and comprehensive organizing force in American culture."[6] To nineteenth-century America every individual was as new as Adam. Each was the first man, each the new unfallen. The American experience was like a moulting season, "a gradual sloughing of the old skin," said D. H. Lawrence echoing Thoreau. In philosophic terms the American frontier experience meant the effort to bring one's own spirit into closer approximation to the world spirit animating all things. It was idealism that stretched out into mysticism. Frederick Jackson Turner in his essay of 1893 called it "a gate of escape from the bondage of the past"—the bondage, one might add, not only of history and institutions but also of human finitude itself. A wall had been broken, a door opened. Out beyond lay a land where "waters ran clear . . . free grass waved a carpet over the face of the earth, and America's man on horseback . . . rode over the rim with all the abandon, energy, insolence, pride, carelessness, and confidence epitomizing the becoming West."[7]

That point at which history becomes myth is that same point at which history becomes meaningful to the human spirit. For it to be taken seriously, all history must contain this mythical element. American frontier history has this element insofar as it expresses something deep within Americans who seek to define their own identity as Americans. Using the poet's language and sharing his vision, Turner described what he thought the significance of the American frontier to be. He saw it as a boundless Eden wherein America's fulfillment would take place. As suggested earlier, Turner's work demands qualification; but as a historian who penetrated to that strange level of myth, he struck something that rang true.

Turner's 1893 essay is doubly important, however, for in it he made the immensely important point that the frontier was now closed. No land now remained to be designated unsettled. Therefore, that vaguely determined line—the frontier—had vanished. But behind this fact lay the far more important truth that with the closing of the frontier came the end of the American myth.

Turner failed to comprehend the full weight of this truth. Actually he thought that even with the frontier closed the old frontier spirit would remain alive; and so in later writing he hailed John D. Rockefeller, Andrew Carnegie, and all other Horatio Algers who, in Turner's view, professed the concomitants to frontierism: free enterprise, laissez-faire, individual rights, natural rights, manifest destiny, popular nationalism, and social mobility. Yet there is something unmistakably ominous in the way Turner begins this essay, first by quoting the census report of 1890 and then by suggesting that this report "marks the closing of a great historic movement." He concludes the essay even more gravely by pointing out that the closed frontier now signals the end of an era that started four centuries earlier with the discovery of America and a hundred years earlier with the Constitution. Indeed, Turner knew America was at a crucial point, but his inveterate optimism shielded him from the tragic sense that darkened Henry Adams's prophetic vision. Nevertheless Turner's announcement suggested that the West was no longer another Eden, that the Westerner was no longer another Adam. The immense implications of an open frontier were now to be eclipsed by those of a closed one. The informing metaphor changed from endless space to the solid wall. Epic changed to tragedy.

The central point regarding the closed frontier is that from this condition develops the necessary climate for tragedy—specifically, for American tragedy. What a closed frontier implies obviously touches other terms by which Americans have sought to understand their development. One thinks, for example, of Adams's symbolic Virgin and Dynamo, or in more recent years of Henry Nash Smith's symbolic Garden and Desert. Henry Steele Commager described this decade of the nineties as "the watershed of American history." Henry F. May called it "the end of American innocence." Van Wyck Brooks used the image of Indian summer, and in his book suggestively entitled *The Machine in the Garden* Leo Marx indicated still another way this important transition in the American experience came about.[8]

What all these terms, including that of a closed frontier, suggest is the end of the Edenic myth and the illusions it fostered. Youth is a time for these illusions, but maturity brings to men and nations the old truths about the tragedy of great expectations. An open frontier was the perfect setting for youthful ambition, for the proud confidence that anything undertaken could be victoriously completed. It was also the place where those breathtaking ideas about the American Adam could be dramatized and where, in short, a new birth of frontier freedom promised an end not only to the bondage of tradition but to the age-old curse of man's original sin. What need was there for the myth of Adam's fall when, in America, Emerson assured his countrymen that through mind alone they could build their own world? "As fast as you conform your life to the pure ideas in your mind," he said, "that will unfold its great proportions." All things disagreeable—"swine, spiders, snakes, pests, madhouses, prisons, enemies"—will vanish until "evil is no more seen."[9] Fortunately for nineteenth-century American literature, Melville, Hawthorne, and James understood the nature of tragedy because they also understood that human evil is not to be annulled by Emersonian fancy. But even more fortunate—and here is an old and perplexing subject —was the fall of Adam, if for no other reason than with it came the birth of tragedy and man's self-understanding.

This kind of knowledge has to do with one's knowing his limitations. He knows himself as man, not as superman or God. He knows himself as finite and as being anxious about this finiteness. Self-understanding comes when he discovers that he has been thrust into the world, not lifted out of it, and that, instead of being newborn, he bears the old scars of his humanity. He dreams of what lies beyond the wall but knows he is doomed to its confinement. He fights to strike through the pasteboard mask but dies in the effort. He crosses the threshold only to find a darker and more entangled one he cannot cross. In the sense of tragedy, this is what it means to "know thyself." It is a self-sought knowledge that one's existence has meaning only within the symbolic walls of a closed frontier.

II

There was little inclination among nineteenth-century Americans to think about tragedy. With an open frontier and its still viable myth, Americans concurred with Thoreau, who reported about his one night in a Concord jail, "I did not for a moment feel confined, and the walls seemed a great waste of stone and mortar."[10] The spirit of the day was one of expansion: a fervent belief that all things were possible—that, for example, Americans could attain eternity, become spirit, and find truth. Whether one's philosophy rested in the dialectic of Hegel or the social evolutionism of Spencer, Americans confidently looked ahead to a time when human problems would disappear and ethics be brought under the triumphant sway of reason.

Tragedy speaks a different language, and it speaks it best within certain walls allowing no escape. This is not to say Americans accepted these walls. On the contrary, their aversion for them equaled their aversion for tragedy. This point needs great emphasis because, as in 1890, many Americans today have not accepted a closed frontier with its national or personal consequences. A long and bizarre chapter in our American history can be written about the ways we have avoided the tragedy implicit in Turner's announcement. Such a chapter must certainly include our messianic role in foreign affairs. Still echoing with American words and bombs is Woodrow Wilson's assertion that the world must be made safe for democracy, as if in this century the world can be made safe for anything. We still innocently interpret history as the children of God going out to battle Satan's armies in what General Dwight Eisenhower called "a great crusade"; and when the Germans and their sympathizers lie defeated, or the Japanese, or the Russians, or the Chinese, or—within our own borders—the Dean Achesons and Owen Lattimores, then the worldwide victory of the American Dream will come to pass.

In different form this Dream is reenacted every day as we sit before our television sets or turn the slick pages of our magazines. Answers to problems require only that we tune in again tomorrow or buy the economy-sized package. A twenty-day Hawaiian cruise promises escape from the treadmill. Hair dyes and diets restore our lost youth. Believing that nothing can frustrate us in the West, we still trek to California, there in the land of sunshine and orange blossoms to find the utopia for which in Iowa we saved our dollars and stock certificates. We attend the Hollywood churches Nathanael West describes in *The Day of the Locust*: the "Church of Christ, Physical," where holiness comes through the use of chestweights and spring grips; the "Church Invisible," where fortunes are told and the dead find lost objects; the "Tabernacle of the Third Coming," where a woman dressed as a man preaches the "Crusade Against Salt"; and the "Temple Moderne," under whose roof "Brain-Breathing, the Secret of the Aztecs," is taught. And with great relief we hear not a word about sin.

Nathanael West's satire on cultists and pathological optimists calls up the peculiarly American penchant for supernaturalism, whether as mysticism, Emersonian transcendentalism, or Mary Baker Eddy's Christian Science. It is important to remember our indebtedness in the nineteenth century to Oriental philosophy with its antipathy toward tragedy. Believing in a symbolically open frontier meant, therefore, transcending human finitude and traveling into those mysterious and supernatural realms beyond this life of clay. It also came to mean a denial of physical reality itself. Certainly nothing auguring the tragic was in Mrs. Eddy's statement in 1875 that there is neither "life, truth, intelligence, nor substance in matter."[11] By contrast tragedy concerns itself not with the invisible world of mystic, saint, or swami, but with the visible world of prisoner and slave. "Who aint a slave? Tell me that," asks Melville's Ishmael. It is a world resembling "a cramped cell," writes Unamuno, "against the bars of which my soul beats its wings in vain." We look out and wish "to merge . . . with the totality of things visible and invisible, to extend [ourselves] into the illimitable of space and to prolong [ourselves] into the infinite of time."[12] But our tragic condition resounds with an everlasting No.

Even after the slaughter of World War I, when it seemed self-evident that something had gone wrong in human affairs, religious liberals in America were determined to muffle this No. Influenced by new findings in Biblical criticism, history of religions, and the psychology of religion, they generally supported the view that Biblical history was itself a movement toward lofty ethical monotheism. They also accepted the nineteenth-century doctrine of progress, which was handily supported by the theory of evolution. The logical step was then to affirm the great moral possibilities of man. Any suggestion that original sin might limit these possibilities was put aside. "If you told the modern American that he is totally depraved," said Santayana in 1911, "he would think you were joking, as he himself usually is. He is convinced that he always has been, and always will be, victorious and blameless."[13] If anything, the war corroborated this judgment, and American religious liberals under the banner of Walter Rauschenbusch went forth to spread the socialized gospel of Christian love. Robert Frost called it "collectivistic regimenting love."[14] Not until Reinhold Niebuhr came onto the scene were the optimistic assumptions of Protestant liberalism successfully challenged.

As for the young artists and intellectuals, their escape from all that a closed frontier implied left them foundering. Some went to Europe where no frontier dream existed. Some simply moved away from their home towns and the puerile Babbittry stifling them. Others went to Greenwich Village in New York or established colonies at Grantwood and Provincetown. Some took up Spiritualism in California's City of Angels. The record has somber personal importance too. Vachel Lindsay committed suicide in 1931; Hart Crane, in 1932; and F. Scott Fitzgerald cracked-up in the late thirties. In the forties Ezra Pound was spared facing trial for treason only because he was adjudged mentally unsound. John Gould Fletcher committed suicide in 1950; Ernest Hemingway, in 1961. The case of Eugene O'Neill may also figure in here, but more testimonial is that of his son, a tall, black-haired man standing six feet three, two hundred and fifteen pounds, with a booming voice and a black beard, a professor of English at Yale, a classical scholar, who at the age of thirty-nine still slept with a teddy bear of childhood days and the same year, 1950, committed suicide with a razor.[15]

Aversion for tragedy explains the passion for escape. When escape is cut off, or when one's lifelong dreams get further and further ahead of one's limitations, the only serious philosophical problem, as Camus said, is suicide. When we find the myth of the open frontier fraudulent and the reality of our confinement too overwhelming to endure, we understand better why it is that of all the American cities with more than 300,000 people, the City of the Golden Gate has the highest rate of suicide. Other Western cities rank close behind. The top five cities with a population of over 100,000, in addition to San Francisco, include Tacoma, Seattle, Sacramento, and Glendale, California. In 1960 Tacoma —on the shores of Puget Sound—ranked first with a rate of 23.7 suicides per 100,000 people, whereas the national average was 10.6. One explanation may be that disillusioned Easterners fail to find their Promised Land on the western frontier that now is closed. In Seattle Dr. Gale Wilson, who performed suicide autopsies at an average of one every two and a half days in 1965, cited what he called "disillusionment with Horace Greeley's 'Go West' command."[16]

Escape from the closed frontier and its demands takes many forms, all of them in a sense suicidal because they either kill life outright or else reduce it to something less than tragic. Physical suicide is only one way to end anxiety

about human finiteness. Another is to falsify the contraries
and opposites of human experience and to settle for comfortable but illusory reconciliation. A person who settles for this
will usually appeal to authority beyond the walls to relieve
the agonizing tensions he finds within them. He seeks to
make the finite infinite, or the infinite finite, and claims to
have broken the walls completely. In Hegelian terms, he
establishes truth in wholeness. But the price he pays is to
neutralize the polarities of good and evil, the divine and
demonic, the light and dark, the thesis and the antithesis—
each otherwise making its independent claims. In neutraliz-
ing paradoxes he also neutralizes human existence, which
is valid only as existence in tragedy. In destroying the walls
he eradicates those "boundary situations" in which we identify ourselves as human within this time and this world.

No wonder that in avoiding tragedy Americans still
look back to a time when the myth assured us no walls
existed, to a time of perpetual youth and innocence. No
wonder that James Reston, in commenting on the 1964
presidential campaign, said that "Mr. Goldwater touches
the deep feeling of regret in American life: regret over the
loss of religious faith; regret over the loss of simplicity and
fidelity; regret over the loss of the frontier spirit of pugna-
cious individuality; regret, in short, over the loss of America's innocent and idealistic youth."[17]

"What we need first and now is to disillusion ourselves," writes Professor Daniel J. Boorstin in *The Image:
or What Happened to the American Dream*. We twentieth-
century Americans, he continues, "suffer primarily not
from our vices or our weakness, but from our illusions."[18]
These are the illusions of youth with its symbolically open
frontier. Coming of age requires the courage to disillusion
ourselves and to accept the fact, as Carl Jung said, that we
"cannot live the afternoon of life according to the pro-
gramme of life's morning—for what was great in the morn-

ing will be little at evening, and what in the morning was true will at evening become a lie."[19] That is, the condition for coming of age is the tragic vision. Specifically referring to America, Van Wyck Brooks defined "coming of age" as the process of outgrowing a simplistic view and instead seeing this nation as a "vast Sargasso Sea" containing "all manner of living things . . . phosphorescent, gayly coloured, gathered into knots and slotted masses, gelatinous, unformed, flimsy, tangled, rising and falling, floating and merging, here an immense distended belly, there a tiny rudimentary brain (the gross devouring the fine)—everywhere an unchecked, uncharted, unorganized vitality like that of the first chaos."[20] The tragic vision cuts through illusions about a past or future Promised Land and takes us into the awesome depth and energy and freedom in this brief, walled-in existence here and now. The tragic heroes need not be kings of Greek or Elizabethan drama; they need be only those persons who, because they are fully attentive to life's contingencies, know and accept themselves for what they are.

III

The concern here is about the climate of tragedy. That the open frontier in America offered no such climate needs the further observation that the closed frontier offers none either, if by it we mean the ironbound world of the determinists. In his well-known discussion of the modern temper, Joseph Wood Krutch was correct in arguing that the triumph of determinism means the defeat of tragedy. Krutch erred, however, in granting the triumph. His central argument in "The Tragic Fallacy" was that the modern temper regards man as nothing more than a pawn, his actions stripped of meaning.[21] If such in fact has happened—and who has not read Aldous Huxley's *Brave New World*?—

then of course Krutch is right. But the writer of tragedy declines to accept the end of man. For him determinism has not triumphed, nor will it so long as man remains the species he presently is. Tragedies, the writer argues, are still to be written, for they come from within the human spirit, not from the outside world of the determinist. It is for this reason that the possibilities for tragedy offer the most hopeful prospect left in this century. Man still trembles in the consciousness that his mortality cuts him off from the whole truth; even so, he has the freedom and pride to seek that truth. At the same time he is conscious that he bears the responsibility for both this freedom and this pride. That he knows this and toils under it is itself a proud idea.

What are the tragedies to be written if the closed frontier serves as the informing metaphor? Fundamental in such tragedy is man of flesh and bone, man in the concrete and profane world. It is not man as idea or as mind or as spirit but rather man who is born, suffers, and dies. All else said thereafter about him comes within the framework of this one fact. Great tragedy accepts this fact and then goes on to tell what happens to man imprisoned by his mortality. It depicts the tragic figure as one who strives to become fully human, to reach out to the limits of his selfhood, in order to claim his full due as a person. "The only fixed star" in the action of tragedy, says Arthur Miller, is "the need of man to wholly realize himself."[22] He awakens to the truth that he is human, and learns through suffering that to be fully human is to be fully tragic. He discovers that suffering, because it is inseparable from tragedy, keeps him human. It allows him no escape to those realms where Keats's nightingale sings eternally. If for a moment his fanciful illusions lift him beyond the walls, suffering brings him back to his "sole self." His song is a *miserere* sung in company with all men who have achieved their full humanity on this side of the wall, the only side where it can be achieved.

With its basic metaphor a closed frontier, tragedy discloses a second condition, namely, the unresolved paradoxes within human life itself. Reason never triumphs here. The Biblical imperative—"Come, let us reason together"—holds little meaning in the world of tragedy where, for example in Miller's *Death of a Salesman,* Linda stands before the fresh grave of her husband Willy and cries, "I search and search and search, and I can't understand it, Willy. I made the last payment on the house today. Today dear. And there'll be nobody home." The play ends with Linda's final and ironic words: "We're free and clear. We're free. We're free . . . We're free. . . ." In O'Neill's *Long Day's Journey into Night* Edmund claims he once knew what it was like to be free—freedom here as transcendence and wholeness. On a ship bound for Buenos Aires he thought the very sky and sea joined in symbolic union, and he with them. Suddenly for him there was peace, "ecstatic freedom," and meaning. Then the veil fell and he was "lost in the fog again." Whether the image is fog, or Van Wyck Brooks's Sargasso Sea, or Henry Miller's "air-conditioned nightmare," the straight way is lost amid the ambiguities of existence. Evil and goodness feed on each other; order and chaos fill the same moment. History records both man's creative and his destructive powers. Art does the same. Man is both far-seeing and blind, free and bound, strong and weak. Reinhold Niebuhr stresses that man stands "at the juncture of nature and spirit."[23] Thus he is neither brute nor angel, neither mere animal nor pure spirit. His glory comes when he reaches the limit of his capacities; at the same time his downfall is assured. His faith is never more human than himself, and thus the tragic tension, "Lord, I believe; help thou mine unbelief." Tragedy holds mutually exclusive polarities in tension. Amid conflict tragedy affirms but never resolves this tension, except in death, which still leaves the same old questions for those who live on.

Even as tragic man comes fully to himself and openly faces the irreconcilable paradoxes, his tragedy is never complete until he confesses what he finds locked within himself. This third element of tragedy requires that he touch the bottom of his own subjectivity, there to find and acknowledge that common birthmark shared by all. The flaw is not in his institutions or in his history except as he is inseparable from them. The flaw of course is what the Greeks called *hubris* and the Christians call sin, and it is in the darkenings of his inner world. Describing this condition Faulkner said that "the heart wants always to be better than it is."[24] Desire is the fatal flaw, and tragedy the freedom to act upon it. The world of tragedy is anthropomorphic, and tragic man is cursed with the desire to make the universe so. He seeks to be larger, better, freer, wiser than himself, and in so doing to solve the riddles, to tame the paradoxes, to shape the "uncreated conscience" of his race. He soars with Icarus and rebels with Prometheus, he builds a tower on the plains of Shinar, and he strides confidently on an open frontier. Desire is the root of his creativity—the desire to leave an enhancing phrase upon the cosmic page. But desire is also the root of his destructiveness, and in the fullness of consciousness he must assimilate the tragic consequences. He sees his desire for immortal fame as also his rage for power, a holy crusade as evil slaughter, reason as madness. And within himself his tragic vision beholds a Lucifer, a wishful "bearer of light," locked in the dungeon of his own heart.

These three qualities—limitation in fullness, paradox, and the flaw—make tragedy possible, just as their discovery marks one's own coming of age. At this point something needs to be said about tragedy and Christianity. Briefly it is this: our need is first tragic, then religious. In America we see the misplaced emphasis that would have the religious spare us from the tragic. "We remain fixated," says Joseph Campbell, "to the unexorcised images of our infancy, and hence disinclined to the necessary passages of our adult-hood."[25] Images of infancy take the form of rebirth, as Turner used the term in his frontier hypothesis, or they may suggest the happy ending of a fairy tale, the mirthful serenity of old age, or the divine comedy of the soul. These conditions, however, come after tragedy because their prerequisite is tragedy. Christianity first serves not as an escape from tragedy but as a mode of entry into it and therefore into what it means to be human. Christianity tells us about fear and trembling; about both peace and the sword; about being forsaken, lost, bewildered, anxious; about having the arrows of God within us. This fullness of consciousness is itself a disease, a death, and therefore a preparation for faith. But faith is theocentric and, to repeat, tragedy is anthropomorphic. Faith validates God-talk, but doubt validates the language of tragedy. This is why tragedy never promises salvation, and it forbids reconciliation between faith and doubt.

The Christian is to believe that faith breaks the wall and opens to him the Kingdom of God. Accordingly, he experiences God as the radically eschatological God. He is thereby freed from the Old Being, the Old Aeon, the Old World, and also from the notion that by understanding this world he understands God. To enter the Kingdom as a New Being means liberation from all the conditions inherent in tragedy. But tragic man knows no final liberation. This is to say he knows no final transcendence because his reference point remains himself.

Strangely enough, modern physics is today underscoring what the tragic poet has been saying since the days of Job. In his book *Modern Science and Modern Man* James B. Conant points out that in the last forty years "physicists have learned to love a situation they once thought to be intolerable," namely, the flux and ambiguity and fragmentation of reality. To those persons who ask what this new outlook means philosophically, Conant quotes the late P. W. Bridgman, professor of physics at Harvard and Nobel Prize winner:

> Finally, I come to what it seems to me may well be from the long range point of view the most revolutionary of the insights to be derived from our recent experiences in physics, more revolutionary than the insights afforded by the discoveries of Galileo and Newton, or of Darwin. This is the insight that it is impossible to transcend the human reference point. . . . The new insight comes from a realization that the structure of nature may eventually be such that our processes of thought do not correspond to it sufficiently to permit us to think about it at all. . . . We are now approaching a bound beyond which we are forever estopped from pushing our inquiries, not by the construction of the world, but by the construction of ourselves. The world fades out and eludes us because it becomes meaningless. We cannot even express this in the way we would like. . . . We are confronted with something truly ineffable. We have reached the limit of the vision of the great pioneers of science, the vision, namely, that we live in a sympathetic world, in that it is comprehensible by our minds.[26]

In Professor Bridgman's autobiography, called *The Way Things Are,* published in 1959, two years before his death, he described what may well be the essence of tragedy when he said that "we never get away from ourselves," nor can the human race as a whole "get away from itself." All our "ostensibly timeless absolutes," all our visions of God's direct intervention are formulated and apprehended by us. "When we talk about getting away from ourselves it is we who are talking. All this is so obvious," he continues, "that it has only to be said, yet it seems to me to have been a major concern of most conventional philosophy and religion to sidestep the consequences of this insight, or not to admit it in the first place."[27]

The tension we know as humans is precisely between our necessity to live in this old world and our desire to break through and beyond to a kingdom of permanence and order. The writer of tragedy denies the possibility of this breakthrough, concurring with Camus that Kierkegaard's "leap of faith" is fallacious. In tragedy man cannot "leap" beyond his own place and time. His test is rather the style by which in this world he lives with himself and others. To Hemingway this style was like a code that permitted no complaining, no appealing. Again it is another modern physicist, J. Robert Oppenheimer, who touched the same tragic note in saying that style "complements affirmation with limitation and with humility" and makes it possible for one "to act effectively, but not absolutely."[28] The tragic hero is a life-stylist, always conscious that tragic limitation keeps the human human and that faith, as the extension of desire, brings to full and magnificent flowering man's fatal flaw.

IV

Yet Americans still insist the frontier is open and, like William Dean Howells in the 1890s, say that the unpleasant and the tragic find more suitable expression in European literature than in American. It is not surprising that Americans took nearly a hundred years to recognize Melville as a tragic writer. The same applies to Hawthorne and Emily Dickinson. The irony is that Europeans have discovered the tragic element in our literature before we have ourselves. But whether in this country or elsewhere, tragedy has always been the antithesis of the popular view. Knowing its unsettling, shattering consequences, Plato prescribed that "the poet shall compose nothing contrary to the ideas of the lawful, or just, or beautiful, or good, which are allowed in the state." He said "a state would be mad" to give free license to the tragedian.[29] Still the Greeks gave the world its greatest tragedies; and, centuries later, despite the almost hysterical insistence that Americans shall continue to stride youthfully on an endless frontier, certain writers have made the tragic journey into the dark forest where the straight way was lost.

Long before Turner made his fateful announcement, James Fenimore Cooper showed that for epical Natty Bumppo the frontier was closed at last, his Edenic sanctuary crudely invaded by the rapacious Ishmael Bush. What Hawthorne wrote concerning man's spiritual malignancy struck even deeper levels of tragedy. As for Melville, his universe consisted of walls, his main effort being to strike through them. His greatest stories, such as *Moby-Dick, Pierre,* "Bartleby the Scrivener," and "The Encantadas," take their structure and meaning from this metaphor. Among writers of this century the tragic vein deeply marks the work of Sherwood Anderson and Ernest Hemingway; Eugene O'Neill, Tennessee Williams, and Arthur Miller; Robert Penn Warren, Flannery O'Connor, and Carson McCullers; Robinson Jeffers and Robert Frost. Most triumphantly it informs the work of William Faulkner, in whose fictional Yoknapatawpha County the smell of honeysuckle, wisteria, and verbena still lingers, suggesting the First Garden; but of more formidable consequence stand the courthouse and the jail, the one testifying to man's rational madness, the other to his tragic gall and travail.

Despite what appears today as a new American fiction in which the Augie Marches, S. Levines, and Burr Fullers "exist in the broad daylight of the post-Freudian [and post-Christian] world, sinless . . . quite cold, beyond comedy, beyond tragedy,"[30] it is unlikely that American writing will permanently shift in this direction. There will always be the tragic artist who sees man as profane, still the man of flesh and bone scarred by his ancient inheritance. Although the artist may sometimes show him differently—as, perhaps, too dead for tragedy or as wholly transfigured by it—his art demands a steadiness of vision wherein he sees himself and those about him still striking at the wall, their crowning curse and tragic flaw still their drudging impulse to straightforwardness in a closed-up world. Great tragic writers come in any age. Melville beheld the closed frontier a half century before Turner announced it. But with the announcement came a peculiar corroboration and a renewed possibility for American tragedy. Americans had spent two centuries pushing back the wall or denying its existence. Perhaps in the 1890s, like Humpty Dumpty, they sat on top of it. But also, like him, they came of age through a tragic fall, and the lesson is there to learn:

> All the king's horses and all the king's men
> Couldn't put Humpty Dumpty together again.

Humpty Dumpty still struggles, and in that pain and pride is his nobility. But the wall still stands. Perhaps a man's only immortality is what he writes on it. Perhaps in some mysterious way it is through the tragedy he there records that he shall come to know the comedy that is divine.

Among several nineteenth- and twentieth-century American writers whose works illustrate the tragedy of the closed frontier, three novelists in particular afford valuable study. With Mark Twain, Ole Rölvaag, and Nathanael West, the American frontier dream clashes with the tragedy of those people who acted upon this dream. What emerges testifies to the fact that as fundamental as the frontier was to the national experience, so too was the tragedy.

II

4

Huckleberry Finn as Tragedy

I

Whatever the difficulties in defining tragedy—either as a literary mode or as a way of looking at life—readers of *Huckleberry Finn* have been wary of calling this American classic a tragedy. Why this should be the case may be inherent in the novel itself, or it may be that Americans in general are reluctant to see anything American as tragic. Unquestionably the nineteenth century gave us a great literary tragedy in *Moby-Dick,* and there may be no debate that Melville's next novel, *Pierre,* or Hawthorne's *Scarlet Letter* deserve similar judgment. But to many readers Mark Twain's masterpiece has seemed in some way too shapeless for tragedy, too lacking in height or depth, too humorous;

and Huck Finn, on both land and river, too elusive to call a tragic hero.

Reluctance to see Twain's novel as tragedy leads to some interesting speculation nevertheless. Henry Nash Smith, for example, notes (italics are mine) that "what had begun as a comic story developed *incipiently* tragic implications contradicting the premises of comedy." Time and again Professor Smith comes close to his own premise of tragedy, then draws back. He says that whereas the "vernacular persona is an essentially comic figure; the character in Huck's meditation is *potentially* tragic." He observes in Huck "a melancholy *if not exactly* tragic strain," yet notes, again with qualification, that what Twain had on his hands in the last part of the novel was "a hybrid—a comic story in which the protagonists have acquired *something like* tragic depth." All the business on the Phelps plantation Professor Smith regards as a "maneuver by which Mark Twain beats his way back from *incipient* tragedy to the comic resolution called for by the original conception of the story."[1]

This same critical ambivalence characterizes what many other readers have discovered about the novel. They reach far enough to find the conditions for tragedy; they may use the terms "tragic" or "tragedy," but they also back away, leaving undeveloped what they have implied. T. S. Eliot suggests "there is no more solitary character in fiction," comparing Huck with Ulysses, Faust, Don Quixote, Don Juan, and Hamlet. Yet, says Eliot, Huck is no tragic figure; a tragic ending to the novel "would reduce [Huck] to the level of those whom we pity."[2] Richard Chase agrees that a tragic conclusion would be inappropriate for Huck, though Chase points out not only that Huck's world is a pattern of "contentment and horror" but that Huck himself knows "the real world with a tragic awareness."[3] James M. Cox argues that Huck's initiation into society carries with it both "tragic irony" and Huck's own "inner awareness" that such membership will destroy his character and deny his values.[4] On the other hand, this awareness is what William C. Spengemann suggests is lacking; nevertheless, in juxtaposing the ideal and the real, innocence and evil, the book contains, he says, "the stuff of tragedy."[5] Still another example of critical ambivalence comes in W. R. Moses' assertion that in many respects Huck's voyage resembles Dante's in the *Inferno*: Huck is "involved in evil, fights against it and suffers under it as a hero should and must." "Yet," says Moses, "he is a *boy,* "and "it would *not* be appropriate for the American waif to bear the ultimate burden of the tragic hero."[6]

These few examples, to which others could be added, serve to point out the difficulties in one's claiming that *Huckleberry Finn* is an American tragedy. It perhaps can be more easily argued that Mark Twain himself was a tragic figure and then let biography carry the burden of tragedy in the novel. Van Wyck Brooks has given an unforgettable picture of Twain's tortured conscience, a picture that takes on more crushing impact in Justin Kaplan's biography, *Mr. Clemens and Mark Twain.*[7] To read Kaplan's last three chapters—"Get me out of business!" "Never quite sane in the night," and "Whited sepulchre"—is to encounter a truly dark, divided, and tragic human being. It is curious, therefore, that some readers who hold back their judgment about *Huckleberry Finn* as tragedy justify their restraint by suggesting that Mark Twain was afraid to write tragedy—or, more precisely, that he was reluctant to develop the tragic implications that stole into what he intended to be a comic story. He had to beat his way back, says Professor Smith, to avoid being engulfed by complexities far beyond his original plan.

We know Twain took seven years to write this book. We know from Walter Blair's study that even though Twain's public success and affluence steadily increased during this period, he was plagued by personal misfortunes, literary failures, the Whittier Birthday fiasco, and, most importantly, by his disillusionment with nothing less than humanity itself.[8] We can only guess the psychological unrest tormenting Twain at this time, perhaps best seen in *The Prince and the Pauper,* written between 1877 and 1881, approximately midway between the start and finish of *Huckleberry Finn.* But to accept Leo Marx's claim that Huck's quest never brought him to a full tragic vision because Twain himself suffered "failure of nerve"[9] is not only to bind the novel irrevocably to the author's biography but also to gloss over the novel's tragic elements. It may be that Twain could not help himself, once he had created Huck and probed into his complex and many-layered inner life, there to discover the tragic fact that Huck, in order to survive in society, had to repress his anxieties and live on the Tom Sawyer surfaces. When through a mistake Aunt Sally Phelps gives Tom's name to Huck, the central irony emerges: "It was like being born again," says Huck, "I was so glad to find out who I was."[10] The novel's whole last section, from Chapter 32 on, is a dramatic travesty of this rebirth, of Huck's becoming Tom. The tragedy rests in the irony that only as Tom can Huck survive. As Tom, Huck has the necessary armor of untruth to safeguard his vulnerable self within. When his identity is at last revealed in Chapter 42, Huck as Huck can no longer stay around. Twain therefore entitles the next (and last) chapter, "Nothing More to Write." For Huck to be adopted and civilized by Aunt Sally means the death of something within himself.

II

The travesty of rebirth is part of a sequence that portrays Huck as a double. One side of his nature is rebellious, intuitive, spontaneous; the other side is logical and fully acculturated. These two sides manifest their equivalents in two kinds of conscience, one constantly troubled by human problems, the other troubled by abstract, impersonal ones. One side is the real Me; the other side the social Me, or what Emerson called the Not Me. The point is that both sides are very much real, both are in conflict with each other; and if reconciliation between the two occurs, it will be the former that yields to the latter.

We see Huck as a Tom figure at the beginning of the novel. As early as the second paragraph we learn that his effort to rebel against Widow Douglas and her civilizing ways has been only short-lived: that although he "lit out" Tom has persuaded him to return on the condition that if he "would go back to the widow and be respectable," he would be allowed to join the "band of robbers." "So I went back," Huck confesses. His commitment to Tom's code spells his death as Huck. For the code, written by Tom and sworn to by all members of the band, demands total allegiance regardless of the duties exacted and foretells the dreadful consequences should those duties not be followed. The oath

> swore every boy to stick to the band, and never tell any of the secrets; and if anybody done anything to any boy in the band, whichever boy was ordered to kill that person and his family must do it, and he mustn't eat and he mustn't sleep till he had killed them and hacked a cross in their breasts, which was the sign of the band. And nobody that didn't belong to the band could use that mark, and if he did he must be sued; and if he done it again he must be killed. And if anybody that belonged to the band told the secrets, he must have his throat cut, and then have his carcass burnt up and the ashes scattered all around, and his name blotted off the list with blood and never mentioned again by the gang, but have a curse put on it and be forgot forever.

It was to this oath—which resembles something as old as the medieval church's curse of excommunication and as modern as fascism, the KKK, and *1984*—that Huck pledged himself in blood. "I made my mark on the paper," he again confesses, not unlike Ishmael, who, pledging total commitment to Ahab and the crew, admitted, "my shouts had gone up with the rest; my oath had been welded with theirs."

We begin to see Huck's other side after he kills himself as a Tom figure. Up to the time he fakes his own murder to escape Pap (Chapter 7), he conforms reasonably well to society's expectations. At first he hated school, but "by and by I got so I could stand it." He says that the longer he went to school "the easier it got to be." He admits he even "was getting sort of used to the widow's ways," and the widow thought he was "doing very satisfactory." And even when Pap forces him away, holding him prisoner in the shack, Huck admits that "it warn't long after that till I was used to being where I was, and liked it—all but the cowhide part." But depicting Pap not only as the worst kind of social racist but also as a victim of delirium tremens gave Twain the opportunity to justify Huck's fake ax-killing. The significance of this death, however, is not that it allows Huck, as a Tom figure, to escape from Pap, but that it frees Huck to become Huck. In different terms, what he earlier killed of himself when he swore allegiance to Tom can now be reborn.

It must be made clear that this rebirth, a process in the novel extending roughly from Chapter 8 to Chapter 31, is radically different from the one described in Chapter 32, entitled "I Have a New Name" and referred to above. Being born again as Tom Sawyer, in Chapter 32, was "easy and comfortable." It made him feel "pretty comfortable all down one side," but the fact that it also made him feel "pretty uncomfortable all up the other" reminds us that in the preceding chapter Huck had finally arrived at his unequivocal fullness as Huck, an experience leaving him *un*easy and *un*comfortable, to say the least. From Chapter 8 on, Huck Finn, as a double, struggles with his own death angel no less than did Pap, and his freedom from it in Chapter 31 marks him as a tragic hero who for a moment stands triumphant over social and moral entanglements but who, too soon, will again be imprisoned by them.

This emergence of Huck as a radically reconstituted personality—as one authentically reborn—begins only after he has committed himself not to a code but to a person. This commitment to Jim and to his safety ironically frees Huck to find and to know himself. Thus Nigger Jim is the means of Huck's deliverance, much as the pagan Queequeg is of Ishmael's. Huck and Jim are both refugees from society; both wish for the freedom they romantically associate with nature, specifically the river. On Jackson Island they come together, finding in each other the goodness and love that social codes had stifled. "I warn't lonesome now," says Huck, who, after hearing about Jim's escape, pledges to Miss Watson's runaway slave, "I ain't a-going to tell." This oath in Chapter 8 marks the beginning of Huck's moral struggle, for by welding himself to Jim he calls into question all those social values that had kept them apart.

On the novel's deepest level Huck's brooding misgivings, striking dread into his heart and repeatedly leaving him "in a sweat," come from the freedom he gains when he chooses to love persons rather than follow people. In choosing to give his highest allegiance to Jim, a member of no respectable band, he ironically gains freedom within the hell to which respectability consigns him. Huck's real freedom is not on the raft, idyllic as that life seems. His only real freedom comes when he squarely faces decision within Tom's world and accepts the curse of excommunication that world decrees.

The turmoil taking place in Huck's inner world, like the trauma of birth itself, has its analogue in the vast exterior world. The great artistry of Mark Twain appears in this perfect blend of what Huck sees on the outside and what he feels within. The first clues to this inner condition are supplied by the frightful omens haunting both Huck and

Jim. Throughout the early chapters certain portents terrify one or the other. Spiders, witches, talk of a floating corpse, Pap's foot tracks in the snow, a hair ball, young birds "flying a yard or two at a time and lighting," storms, handling a snakeskin: about such occurrences Huck asks Jim if there were not any good signs. "Mighty few—an' *dey* ain't no use to a body," he answers.

This tone of foreboding becomes more intense during action that takes place on the river. Many readers have thought the contrary: that the river represents an idyllic retreat, a place of perfect freedom and naturalness. Extending this notion further, Philip Young thinks that the river symbolizes "a dark and silent unknown," and that what characterizes Huck's several departures from the land to the river are the qualities of "ease, silence, and darkness."[11] But as Huck's inner world of troubled conscience cannot thus be fully described, neither can the river, the scene again and again of horror, violence, and intrigue— with, for example, the house of death floating by, the killers on board the *Walter Scott,* fog and the separation of Huck and Jim, the steamboat that runs them down, slave hunters, the Duke and the Dauphin, and violent storms. With proper understatement Huck observes that "the raft was a most uncommon lively place."

But it is on the land where Huck's boiling conscience —the conscience concerned with persons rather than abstractions—finds its most telling correlatives. For Mark Twain this was clearly to be the payoff. If he were to delineate Huck as a tragic character—one whose real self must confront the equally real world he lives in—Twain would have to show the boy the worst of his own society, including all those corrupt values that molded him into the boy he culturally was. The tension inherent in Huck's tragic position had to be pulled taut, and whether Twain's reluctance to do this accounted for his putting the manuscript aside after a summer's work of four hundred pages in 1876 remains unknown. Upon the completion of *Tom Sawyer* the previous year he had written to William Dean Howells that he (Twain) had decided not to "take the chap [Tom] beyond boyhood," for ". . . if I went on now and took him into manhood, he would just lie like all the one-horse men in literature and the reader would conceive a hearty contempt for him." "By and by," he continued, "I shall take a boy of twelve and run him on through life (in the first person) but not Tom Sawyer—he would not be a good character for it."[12] To Huck was given the burden of experience's bringing him figuratively into manhood and literally into tragic understanding. It was with Chapter 17 that Twain resumed the novel, adding to it the kind of scathing realism and dark power that puts into sharp relief what Huck is morally in for now that he has pledged himself to Jim. In Chapter 15 that pledge had become totally significant when Huck humbly apologized for tricking Jim into thinking that their separation in the fog was only Jim's dream. This apology, Professor Smith notes, "is striking evidence of growth in moral insight."[13] Chapter 16 then brings Huck face to face with the hard fact that he is actually helping a slave escape. "My conscience got to stirring me up hotter than ever," Huck says. "I was . . . all in a sweat to tell on him. . . . I just felt sick. But I says, I *got* to do it—I can't get *out* of it." By the time Twain finished this chapter and put the manuscript aside, the pattern of the novel was clearly drawn; he had only to summon the courage and to perfect the artistry in order to follow where the novel's tragic design pointed. He did both.

III

There is no need to recount all the shattering experiences Huck underwent each time he stepped off his raft. That he wanted to regard them merely as adventures, after the manner of Tom, suggests an understandable desire to remain detached and therefore unscarred. In carrying out his own fake murder, for example, he said, "I did wish Tom Sawyer was there; I knowed he would take an interest in this kind of business, and throw in the fancy touches." In later boasting to Jim about this same business, he could not resist the observation that "Tom Sawyer couldn't get up no better plan than what I had done." And in persuading an apprehensive Jim to search the wrecked steamboat with him, Huck asked, "Do you reckon Tom Sawyer would ever go by this thing? Not for a pie, he wouldn't. He'd call it an adventure." But what start as adventures to Huck soon become searing realities. He sees the cruelty of river-townsmen; the pathos of broken slave families; the deceit of confidence men, fakers, itinerant evangelists, obscene showmen, masquerading all the while as noblemen; the hypocrisy and vicious feuding of the aristocracy; the bullying of a murderer and the cowardice of a lynching mob; and, woven throughout these episodes, the ever-present reminder of ghosts, corpses, evil omens, and murder. "It was enough to make a body ashamed of the human race," Huck says at one point. "I never see anything so disgusting. . . . it was just sickening," he says another time. Or again: "Well, it made me sick to see it. . . . It was a dreadful thing to see." What he saw was the damned human race, and what he felt was the soul-sickness of one exposed to the fraudulent social basis of his own professed faith.

Matching the courage to run Huck "on through life" was the artistic technique by which Twain sent Huck on this dreadful journey. This technique is marked by the multiple names, disguises, and concealments given to Huck. Professor Donna Gerstenberger notes that the metaphor of disguise in this novel is "disturbing and persistent." She points out that "Huck is never in society *as himself.* He is forced to use one disguise after another to conceal his identity, not only to *escape* but also to *join* society."[14] This observation is valid, though it fails to take into account the tragic paradox that, first, in order to *survive* in society Huck must wear masks, and, second, that masks alone do not insure his survival. It is true that without disguises Huck would be unable to live as Huck. It is equally true that the one disguise he could never effect—the one lie he could never pray—was to regard Jim as only another mask. Sometimes Huck is Tom; he is also Sarah Williams, George Peters, George Jackson, and, hilariously enough, "Sarah Mary Williams George Elexander Peters." Tom is William Thompson and Sid; the two rapscallions are the Duke of Bridgewater and "Looy the Seventeen," later Harvey Wilkes and his brother William; Jim is King Lear as well as a "Sick Arab." All these disguises, and more, suggest a world of masks and games, swindlers and con men, pedigrees and Prufrocks—in short, a chaotic world in which the true and false are indistinguishable except to Huck, who perceives realities within the chaos and who, unmasked, answers when Jim calls him "honey." It is this name, and Huck's precarious freedom to respond to it, that means his survival as Huck.

To suggest this crazy fabric of societal life, Mark Twain supplies more than disguises, hoaxes, schemes, and pseudonyms. As technique, nothing is more fundamental to the novel than its irony—an irony by which Twain takes his readers to the heart of tragedy. From the title itself we get our earliest clue; we learn, as mentioned before, that Huck's "adventures" were experiences of the most shattering intensity. Tom has no understanding of this fact. When the two boys meet on the Phelps farm, Tom wants to know "all about" what had befallen Huck because, to Tom, "it was a grand adventure, and mysterious, and so it hit him where he lived." "But," Huck said to him, "leave it alone till by and by," knowing that the real "adventures" of Huckleberry Finn he could never share.

Irony deepens as Huck and Jim escape to the river. This is not the same Mississippi River Twain wrote about in the seven sketches of 1875 for the *Atlantic Monthly* and published the same year as *Old Times on the Mississippi.* In that earlier book the river is an object external to Twain, age forty. Even though he describes it affectionately and acknowledges its "eluding and ungraspable" quality, the river is still outside his creative imagination, still either the river of traditionally romantic associations or else the river where he once learned to pilot a steamboat. Perhaps one can argue that the book does symbolically describe a rite of initiation into the river's dangerous and intricate ways. Yet the powerful, tragic overtones are clearly absent, nor are they found in the enlarged version of 1882, *Life on the Mississippi,* a book Twain intended as little more that a travelogue, eliciting from him a few days after he finished it the fierce comment: "I will not interest myself in *any* thing connected with the wretched God-damned book."[15] No, the Mississippi River that Mark Twain imaginatively created for his masterpiece is clearly a different river from that found in the earlier two books. The river Huck and Jim flee to holds mythic terrors as profound as the superstition-ridden psychic depths of its travelers. At night its fateful currents take Jim beyond Cairo, where he supposedly was to have found freedom, and into ever more hostile country where, eventually, he will be turned in by the king "for forty dirty dollars." Where the river will take Huck is implied in the last scene Twain wrote before he put the manuscript away. Coming upstream was a steamboat, pounding ever closer in the darkness, its form looking like "a black cloud with rows of glow-worms around it; but all of a sudden she bulged out, big and scary, with a long row of wide-open furnace doors shining like red-hot teeth." As the fiery monster smashed through the raft, Huck dived into the black water, his escape serving ironically as a ritual of baptism. "I aimed to find the bottom," he said, an ominous indication of what awaits him.

All the terrors and nightmares of hell evoked by the river are not to be forgotten even when, at the beginning of

Chapter 19, we come to a description many readers, including Ernest Hemingway, have justifiably regarded as one of the most beautifully lyrical paeans Mark Twain ever wrote about the river.[16] Demonic blackness has now become an ethereal radiance as the dawn spreads its gentle light over the river, from whose banks blows a breeze "so cool and fresh and sweet to smell on account of the woods and flowers." It could almost be the river Ganges, the water as sacramental as Walden Pond, the morning as beatific as when Billy Budd met the dawn of his transfiguration. There is now no desperate plunge into the water's depths; instead, Huck and Jim "slid into the river and had a swim, so as to freshen up and cool off," and then "set down on the sandy bottom where the water was about knee-deep, and watched the day-light come."

The river is both benign and treacherous, and it is this conflict between the two that gives ironic density to the novel, not wholly unlike the irony of Melville's masterpiece in which we learn that the most dreaded creatures of the sea glide hidden beneath the loveliest surface tints of blue. Each aspect of the river must be recognized, especially that which T. S. Eliot in the *Four Quartets* called the "implacable," that quality serving as a "reminder of / What men choose to forget."

The same irony obtains in Huck's innocence or naturalness. Typical of those readers who accept the literalness of Huck's innocence is Gladys Bellamy's remark that Huck is "the 'natural man,' " suggesting to her "Walt Whitman's dream of the great American who should be simple and free."[17] But Huck—much closer to Melville than to Whitman—is neither simple nor free, and his innocence has a dark side not unlike that of the river. James Cox says it is the inscrutable Pap who puts Huck "in touch with the deeper human forces."[18] It is Jim, however, who tells Huck about these forces within Pap and, most importantly, within Huck himself. Jim does this through a crucial prophecy he

70 *The Closed Frontier*

interprets from the hair ball in Chapter 4. The prophecy
tells about two angels hovering around Pap, one white and
the other black. "De white one gits him to go right a little
while, den de black one sail in en bust it all up. . . . A body
can't tell yit which one gwyne to fetch him at de las'." As for
Huck, Jim continues:

> You gwyne to have considable trouble in yo' life, en
> considable joy. Sometimes you gwyne to git hurt, en
> sometimes you gwyne to git sick; but every time you's
> gwyne to git well ag'in. Dey's two gals flyin' 'bout you
> in yo' life. One uv 'em's light en t'other one is dark. One
> is rich en t'other is po'. You's gwyne to marry de po'
> one fust en de rich one by en by. You wants to keep
> 'way fum de water as much as you kin, en don't run no
> resk, 'kase it's down in de bills dat you's gwyne to get
> hung.

The prophecy not only warns what will befall Huck but
makes as explicit as any other statement in the novel the
ironic nature of both Huck and the river. If innocence and
benign naturalness were all there was to be found, then the
whole possibility of tragedy would disappear. But Twain's
view of life is tragic, which means that life is synonymous
with conflict, just as conflict is the essence of irony. Perhaps
irony overreaches itself when Twain has tragic insights
come to a seemingly innocent boy whose awareness can
hardly be expected to encompass the full meaning of
tragedy. This argument, however, fails to take into account
the myth of the American Adam who represents reborn innocence. This is the myth Twain emphatically destroys in
the novel. Huck's painful rebirth, which culminates in Chapter 31, does not deliver him from a world of complexity and
finiteness but, instead, thrusts him squarely into it. His is
the loss of innocence, not the American Adam's recovery of
it. His is the decision to be a man, not the Adamic freedom

to remain a child. To Huck comes the tragic, un-Wordsworthian realization that the man *is* the father of the child.

IV

At the heart of the novel is the question of freedom, though not the kind of freedom readers have commonly associated with Huck's flight to the river. The central metaphor is neither the river, the land, nor all those ploys connected with the metaphor of disguise. With profound irony the theme of freedom comes through the metaphor of prison. Thus we see that Jim the slave is the freest of men; whereas Tom, the perfect representative of what society calls freedom, is bound by the invisible chains of custom and tradition. Neither Jim nor Tom "sweat" over their identity: the one knows he is a slave and thereby possesses that secret if unconscious wisdom of his own freedom; the other knows he is free and thereby lives deluded as to his real enslavement. Jim is Jim and Tom is Tom, their occasional disguises causing them no anxiety, their respective conditions of freedom and imprisonment leading to no conscious ambivalence. The tragic figure is Huck who knows both the freedom of conscience and the bondage of convention, who lives through the terrible cycles of death and rebirth and death again, who at the end of the novel learns he has won $6000 but lost a father, and who still fatefully seeks the freedom of some illusory open frontier, even after he has experienced the only freedom he will ever know—the freedom within what Melville called "a joint stock company of two": Ishmael and Queequeq bound together: Huck and Jim, free to love only within the strictures of their society.

Huck achieves freedom within this social framework, not outside or beyond it. This freedom has meaning only as it is inseparable from his condition as a child of culture.

Huck's famous declaration of independence in Chapter 31 paradoxically occurs at that moment when his individuality —won at so great a struggle—merges with that of Jim. At such a moment in *Moby-Dick* Ishmael's free will was dealt "a mortal wound." So too was Huck's, and the same tragic irony is in Huck's cry, "All right, then, I'll go to hell," the hell of social disgrace in which the grace of love can flourish.

This then is Huck's true rebirth, and Randall Stewart is right in calling it one of the greatest moments in all American literature.[19] But what then of the last twelve chapters? Does the unity of the work break down when Tom comes into the foreground to engineer Jim's elaborate escape? Are these chapters Mark Twain's comic way of avoiding the tragic?

With the prison as the novel's key metaphor—plus all the imagery, situations, and meanings associated with it in the novel—these last twelve chapters are indispensable to Twain's tragic meaning. That we are prepared for his use of this metaphor long before it dominates the last third of the novel is important, for we see it as an extension and enlargement of earlier situations. Miss Watson hems in Huck with endless restrictions: "Don't put your feet up there, Huckleberry"; "Don't scrunch up like that, Huckleberry"; "Don't gap and stretch like that, Huckleberry." Illustrations abound to show Huck's freedom tightly limited by his social context and historical heritage. In this connection Huck's clothes aptly symbolize this bondage, for whenever he could he went naked, "day and night," the new clothes the Grangerfords made for him being "too good to be comfortable." Of course Huck was also physically imprisoned by Pap. And, in a sense, he was entangled by all those undelineated forces in his psychic life, not only by the vast web of superstitions but also by dreams of violence and murder that, he said, "I ain't ever going to get shut of." As for Jim, the institution of slavery made certain what his limitations were. Both

Huck and Jim are prisoners, each tells the other of his escape when the two first meet on Jackson Island, and throughout their odyssey the constant need to escape one tight squeeze after another serves to emphasize their confinement. The freedom to be himself that Huck achieves in Chapter 31 echoes Melville's reminder in *Mardi* that "Freedom is the name for a thing that is *not* freedom." Huck's freedom is meaningful only through the tragic fact that he remains a prisoner of his culture, a fact about which the novel's last twelve chapters leave no doubt.

In the first of these last chapters Huck has only to set foot on the Phelps plantation to wish he were dead and "done with it all." His wish is soon granted when Aunt Sally calls him Tom. As Huck, he has known self-reliance; but this condition leaves him too exposed, too free, and he therefore must die in order to be reborn as Tom, symbolic of his necessary and inevitable reentering the prison-house of Tom's world. Huck's willingness to obey Tom's "Dark, Deep-laid Plans" in Chapter 35 recalls his swearing to Tom's "dark oath" in Chapter 2. In both instances he resigns himself to the rules Tom twines around him.

Huck's own plans to steal Jim from the custody of Silas Phelps are simple and straightforward, but for this reason they have no place among the belittered difficulties Tom invents. The finality of Tom's ways squeezes unequivocally upon Huck. Tom says, "It don't make no difference how foolish it is, it's the *right* way—and it's the regular way. And there ain't no *other* way, that ever *I* heard of, and I've read all the books that gives any information about these things." Tom's intricate strategy is matched only by the tools he demands for the job: candles and candlesticks, a sheet, a spoon, a shirt, case-knives, a rope ladder, shovels, an undecipherable coat of arms, inscriptions for Jim to write on rock, a grindstone, rattlesnakes for Jim to tame, rats and spiders, a warming pan, a "witch-pie," a flower for

Jim to water with his tears, "nonnamous letters," and so on. Within this fantastic network Tom himself is in high spirits. Huck observes "it was the best fun he ever had in his life, and the most intellectural," Tom wanting nothing more than to "keep it up all the rest of our lives and leave Jim to our children to get out."

As for Jim, Huck knows "he couldn't see no sense in the most of it, but he allowed we was white folks and knowed better than him; so he was satisfied, and said he would do it all just as Tom said." Tom's game leaves Jim's deeper self untouched. With complete acceptance Jim remarks, "I never knowed b'fo' 'twas so much bother and trouble to be a prisoner." Tom's news that Miss Watson had set Jim free in her will two months beforehand only corroborates what Jim's real condition has been throughout the novel. He has been free all along in the sense that his sorrow, compassion, joy, and love sprang genuinely and unambiguously from his individual humanity. Tom, on the other hand, is so entrapped by his own game that he allows for no expression of feelings that might identify his humanity with someone else's. The chilling horror of this fact is not only that Tom, when wounded by a bullet, remains insensitive to the love behind Jim's all-night ministrations, but that to Tom life itself is nothing more than a game in which rules take precedence over persons. Jim's plight is never anything but an abstraction to Tom. All the stratagems for freeing Jim actually keep the two apart. The icy impersonality required by the game is best seen when Tom explains why he superintended Jim's escape, all the while knowing that Miss Watson had freed him. "Why," he said, "I wanted the *adventure* of it; and I'd 'a' waded neck-deep in blood to —— [have it?]." What better justification do we have for the "computerized" adventure we now call war?

Where is Huck within the maze of these last chapters? He takes his stance between the person of Jim and the persona of Tom, between the assertive and personal forces from within and the inhibiting, impersonal forces from without, between individual freedom and social rule. His is a tragic stance requiring that he compromise with what Henry Adams called the "perplexing, warring, irreconcilable problems, irreducible opposites." "From earliest childhood," Adams wrote in his *Education,* he "was accustomed to feel that, for him, life was double." The same insight comes to Huck who, as a double, discovers that only by killing something within himself can he live in this world. His resolution is never static. Appalled by Tom's sense of adventure as a mere game, Huck is also a little beguiled by it. Embracing the individuality of Jim, he still feels the hard truth Melville's Babbalanja voiced: "to be, is to be something." The "something" Jim was, was a Negro, a slave, a socially consigned inferior. Unlike Melville's Pierre, who learned "that unless he committed a sort of suicide as to the practical things of this world, he never can hope to regulate his earthly conduct by that same heavenly soul," Huck Finn learns the contrary: that unless he kills something of his soul, he can never live amid the practical things of this world. To Huck there are no cosmic sanctions, no metaphysics, no "strange brown god," no Aristotle, Hegel, or Wordsworth to posit unity and wholeness. Even more significantly, there is no Whitman, no American Dream, no open frontier. There is only the world he lives in but never made.

What makes this novel important in the development of American tragedy is that we see for the first time the meaning of America's closed frontier. Huck's journey does not take him to the stars but only into the hell of his own civilization, from which there is no safety valve of escape. At this point of no exit we see the fierce collision between what the American Dream promised and what the inexorable limitations of the closed frontier set down. Spiritual deliverance collided with moral finiteness; or, more to the point in Twain's novel, democratic ideals of selfhood collided with social realities. The frontier spirit represented by the pioneer's singular courage and enterprise had become infected, so that, as Floyd Stovall remarks, "the builder was imprisoned by the edifice he built."[20] All that is left in such a prison is one's own personality. Karl Jaspers suggests that "in acting out" one's personality, in realizing one's selfhood "even unto death," one finds his only deliverance.[21] For a crucial moment Huck found this deliverance, this new birth; but what makes his existence tragic is the fact that, as Northrop Frye says, "every new birth provokes the return of an avenging death. . . . On one side of the tragic hero is an opportunity for freedom, on the other the inevitable consequence of losing that freedom."[22] So it is with Huck Finn. To him the lesson of tragedy taught possibility as well as limitation.

This irony touches the last two sentences of the novel. For Huck the possibility still exists "to light out for the territory ahead of the rest." In this Indian Territory, later to become Oklahoma, Huck hopes to rediscover that moment of deliverance like the one he experienced with Jim. His fate is to hope he can stay "ahead of the rest." Though he once found his freedom among them, he continues to search for it beyond. A final and cryptic postscript to this tragic fate comes in the brief entry Twain wrote in his notebook in 1891 (contemplating an extension of the Tom-Huck story): "Huck comes back sixty years old, from nobody knows where—and crazy."[23]

5

The Tragic Trilogy
of Ole Rölvaag

I

In *Their Fathers' God,* the third volume of Ole Rölvaag's trilogy of the American prairie, Peder Holm asks
Nikoline Johansen, "What is *hilder* like?" Newly arrived
from Norway and soon to return, Nikoline explains to
American-born Peder that *hilder* is a mirror-like mirage
appearing in the sky on certain Norwegian summer nights
when the air is "clear and warm and still." The islands off
the northern coast "stand on their heads in the air—they
just float there. The ships sail with their masts pointing
down; up in the sky you understand. Oh, you can't imagine
how beautiful such nights are! . . . It's a fairyland and you
aren't a bit afraid. . . . All space is a magic mirror . . . you

see only phantasms floating in a great stillness . . . you don't dare breathe for fear they'll pass away" [ellipses Rölvaag's]. When Peder says that life in America is a *hilder,* Nikoline distinguishes between the American and the Norwegian: "We know when we see *hilder,*" she said; "we can tell it and make allowance. You Americans believe all you see until you run your heads against a stone wall; then you don't believe anything any more." "You're an American," she added, "you saw *hilder* and believed it."[1]

Fundamental to the American experience are these phantasms, these often vague but nonetheless compelling dreams that beckoned the immigrant and the pioneer to build a kingdom or, at best, to make his house a castle. But from these same dreams came the inevitable tragedy, most dramatically symbolized by the closed frontier. The basic fact about the American experience is the tragedy inherent in it, a tragedy Americans even yet have not fully assimilated: that with every dream of freedom there is the conflicting actuality of limitation; that with every absolute —be it equality, justice, human dignity—there is a tragic contradiction. After every *yes,* there is a *no.* Among the greatest idealists in American literature a slender thread of tragedy appears. Even Emerson found his philosophical scheme incomplete until he had written "Experience" and "Fate," and had lived in what he called "the house of pain." Among the less great—especially among those who make the public pronouncements intended for the popular mind —the absence of this tragic thread indicates ignorance of the American experience rather than optimism about it. As for the Norwegian-born Ole Edvart Rölvaag, his writing combines the themes of both freedom and fate, of society and solitude, of kingdom-building and its awesome price. What his fictional trilogy—*Giants in the Earth* (1927), *Peder Victorious* (1929), and *Their Fathers' God* (1931)—makes clear is that to see *hilder* and once to believe it is to learn the lesson of American tragedy.

By the time Rölvaag joined the St. Olaf College faculty in 1906, ten years after he first arrived in this country as a twenty-year-old immigrant, he was persuaded that two powerful forces had shaped American life. These were Immigration and the Westward Movement. He could number himself part of the first, writing in his journal on July 29, 1896: "It is done; it is done. I have left home."[2] Only imaginatively could he count himself a western pioneer, though doing so was not difficult in Elk Point, South Dakota, where he arrived in September and immediately experienced prairie life as "monotonous and without depth and nuances."[3] Yet as he went on to earn his diploma (with honors) from Augustana Academy in Canton in 1901 and his bachelor's degree four years later from St. Olaf College, he began to see something epical in both Immigration and the Westward Movement. To Rölvaag the immigrants in the 1840s and after resembled Vikings, acting out their part in a great national epic. Though he mainly testified for the Norwegian immigrants, Rölvaag interpreted this entire movement west as the expression of purposive and heroic idealism, as singleness of will. Addressing students in 1907 he said that such singleness of will, if it is to remain total, must aim at "the good," and, finally, it must be brought into harmony with the singleness of God's will.[4] It was, then, in this way that Rölvaag challenged his youthful students and conceived his own purpose. In a larger view he applied the same tone, if not terms, to the American frontier experience. Writing some twenty years later of it, he said that the pioneers "threw themselves blindly into the Impossible and accomplished the Unbelievable. . . . Not since the day man first took up his struggles has the human race known such faith and a like confidence—once more the race had been made young!"[5]

Such idealism colors Rölvaag's teaching and public addresses. On his deeper and more creative levels, however, his imagery of pioneers as Israelites and of the West as

Canaan gives way to an Ibsen-like gloom, to a hovering sense of fatality. The central problem Rölvaag faced was whether to write an American epic or an American tragedy. Through the character of Per Hansa in *Giants in the Earth* Rölvaag had created an epical Moses figure. Per Hansa had led his family across the wilderness; at Spring Creek he had founded a Norwegian settlement that to him was a kingdom, and he had envisioned his own grand estate—his royal mansion, magnificent barn, and endless fields of golden wheat. "The palace itself would be white, with green cornices . . . the big barn would be as red as blood, with cornices of driven snow."[6] Per Hansa's "divine restlessness" would keep him forever striding forward "with outstretched arms toward the future." Little matter that on the verge of fulfillment he would die, like Moses; for like the great patriarch, Per Hansa would have a successor, his own son, Peder Victorious, who, in the last novel of the trilogy, will echo his father: "Our task is here to build up happiness so great and so wonderful that the glory of it will brighten up the far corners of the world."

Had Rölvaag chosen to write his trilogy as epic, he would have had to portray action commensurate with the idealism engendered by the myth of the West. This of course he did in the character of Per Hansa, whom one critic has compared with Odysseus.[7] But it must be quickly added that Per Hansa dies a third of the way through the trilogy. Furthermore, the reader begins to suspect only halfway through the first book that Per Hansa, despite his stature as a western hero, will not triumph, and, in fact, the forces of fate will verify only too clearly Pascal's observation that "man is but a reed, the feeblest thing in Nature."[8] The chapter titles concluding the first book are ominous enough: "Facing the Great Desolation," "The Heart That Dared Not Let in the Sun," "On the Border of Utter Darkness," "The Power of Evil in High Places," and, finally, "The Great Plain

Drinks the Blood of Christian Men and Is Satisfied." Within these chapters Rölvaag allows no sentimentality to mitigate the woe and desperation visited upon the pioneers. One evening, for example, after a three-day fog had finally lifted and the western sun was transforming the clouds into "marvellous fairy castles," Per Hansa's wife, Beret, sat watching a lone wagon slowly moving over the prairie from the northeast. She and Per Hansa were soon to discover that inside the wagon, which was bearing a pitiable family of four, the mother crouched with her wrists bound with strong rope to the handles of a large immigrant chest; so insane with grief was she after burying her small son behind on the prairie that Jakob, her husband, could restrain her delirium only with rope. To Per Hansa the woman looked as if she had been "crucified." In telling his story, Jakob could say little more than "Fate just willed it so. . . . It isn't any use to fight against Fate."

Although Per Hansa, his progeny, and his fellow pioneers will physically master the wilderness, as Frederick Jackson Turner described the frontiersmen's eventual triumph, other incidents in these final chapters of *Giants* suggest that more powerful forces are at work than those with which the Norwegian, as epic hero, can cope. Physical desolation caused by locusts season after season leaves Per Hansa outraged and bewildered, not only because the crops were ruined but because he found it "impossible to outguess" the deadly insects. "No creatures ever acted so whimsically or showed such a lack of rational, orderly method. One field they might entirely lay waste, while they ate only a few rods into the next; a third, lying close beside the others, they might not choose to touch at all." Even more baffling to Per Hansa is Beret's oncoming insanity. He can do nothing to overpower her feelings of psychological desolation, loneliness, exile; her certainty that an inexorable destiny possesses her life; her guilt for having conceived

Peder out of wedlock; her anguish as she secretly prepares the family chest for her own coffin, in which Per Hansa later finds her, still breathing but tightly coiled like a foetus. The most mysterious force is death itself, ironically claiming Per Hansa on the same winter day that he thinks about the barn he would build next fall—"a real show barn," he called it. Like the rich man in the Gospel of St. Luke whose soul was demanded even while he dreamed of bigger barns to hold his wealth, Per Hansa dies close to the edge of the same dream. That his frozen body faced west when found the following spring is one of many ironies underlying the trilogy.

II

Percy Boynton once observed that Rölvaag's novels had come at a good time—at a time, that is, when the long accumulation of frontier literature was accepted as corroboration of Turner's frontier thesis. Boynton's point, however, was not that Rölvaag continued in the tradition of James Fenimore Cooper, William Gilmore Simms, Timothy Flint, James Hall, Edward Eggleston, Joseph Kirkland, and William Allen White—all frontier novelists of sorts. Nor did he interpret Rölvaag as one who depicted the process of Americanization according to the thesis Turner laid down. Instead, what he saw in Rölvaag's work was the Westerner not as a conqueror of the frontier but as one conquered by it.[9] Boynton failed to trace the implications in Turner's statement that the frontier was closed, but he did assert that Rölvaag had significantly shifted away from the idealistic myth that the frontiersmen's triumph vindicated the American Dream.

Closer to Rölvaag's treatment of the Westerner, especially the newly transplanted European, are Willa Cather's *O Pioneers* and *My Ántonia.* But in the case of both Alexandra Bergson and Ántonia Shimerda, the indomitable heroines in these novels, Willa Cather idealized the immigrant. As a "Nebraska-Virginian," Boynton said, she knew her people only through "sympathetic observation," and "when sympathy and observation come into conflict, sympathy triumphs." This meant, according to Boynton, that Willa Cather was unwilling to resign her characters to their fate, and equally unwilling, therefore, to "record the [frontier's] conquest of the pioneers."[10] The same qualification about Cather's work—and that of other frontier writers like Ruth Suckow, Margaret Wilson, and Herbert Quick—supported Vernon Louis Parrington's judgment that Rölvaag, far more than these other writers, displayed "the profound insight and imaginative grasp of theme that gives to *Giants in the Earth* so great a sense of tragic reality."[11]

Still another student of the American West, Henry Steele Commager, called *Giants* "the most penetrating and mature depictment [*sic*] of the westward movement in our literature." But Commager adds that this movement has none of the romanticism associated with a proud epic of man's conquest of earth. In Rölvaag's novels, "the westward movement . . . becomes the tragedy of earth's humbling of man." Of all tragedies, Commager writes, "the most poignant is that of futility. . . . And futility is the moral of *Giants in the Earth.*"[12]

These readers saw *Giants* as unmistakable tragedy, the same genre in which Boynton also included *Peder Victorious,* published the same year (1929) that he wrote his appraisal. What is necessary now is to see the entire trilogy as a frontier tragedy, certainly one of the most sustained in American literature. And if a single symbol informs these three novels, it is again that of the closed frontier, the stone wall that obtrudes in the *hilder* vision, or the magic ring appearing to Beret early in the first novel. This circle lay on the horizon and extended upward into the sky, or, in slightly different imagery, "it was like a chain inclosing the king's garden, that prevented it from bearing fruit. . . . And those who were strong enough to break through were only being enticed still farther to their destruction!"

To Beret this ring represented the border of human exploration, the invisible barrier marking the limits of human finitude. To go beyond—as Per Hansa tried to do—was to trespass into awesome precincts of mystery and to invite one's destruction through pride. This ring also symbolized a psychological border beyond which lay the unknown, the wild, the desolate, and the dark forces of the mind. To go farther west was to intensify these psychological feelings. As Beret knew, the journey west was like getting lost within one's own inner prairies, a far more precarious adventure than fording rivers and fighting snowstorms. Still another significance associated with the closed frontier in this trilogy was that of cultural entanglements, the kind the second-generation immigrant confronted as he learned that his father's utopian dreams of America as a great and democratic "melting pot" had little connection with the dirty business of politics or the sometimes ugly conflicts between differing ethnic and religious groups. The ingenious way Rölvaag presented the overall tragedy was to see it in these three aspects. Per Hansa, closest to an epic figure in his superhuman strength both in working and in dreaming, dies a tragic figure, unfulfilled in either. His tragedy inheres in what he demands of himself in relation to fate, or in relation to the prairies and to their strange and overwhelming might. With his whole heart he summoned the courage to found a kingdom, but in the long run the cosmic powers he sought to conquer were his nemesis, first freezing him in their icy grasp, then leaving him a putrid corpse in the spring thaw. Beret's tragic drama is played out not on the Dakota prairies but, as suggested above, amid those prairies of the mind—"my own desert places," as Robert Frost called them. Try, in *Giants,* as she would to curtain the windows from these dreadful vistas or to keep close to her as protection those few possessions like the trunk she brought from Norway; dream as she would of the old Norwegian churchyard "enclosed by a massive stone wall, broad and heavy"—a wall "more reliable" than anything she could imagine; yet she, who feared the great stillness of the prairies more than anyone and who longed for some kind of wall to hide behind, was bereft of all security except a chill Lutheranism. Hers is the tragedy of deracination, of cultural uprootedness, of separation from language and tradition, without any psychological moorings to compensate.

The tragedy Peder comes to know is the fraudulence of hope in America as a cultural melting pot where immigrants of diverse backgrounds can start anew to build a harmonious society. Peder rebels against old Norwegian traditions. He turns his back on the God of his fathers. Representing the new American whose traditions are only as deep as the American experience itself, Peder carries out his rebellion by marrying Susie Doheny, an Irish Catholic. "Wait until we get to the end of the world," Peder says to her, "then I'll tell you all manner of beautiful things!" "Are we going to the end of the world?" she replies. "Of course we are!"[13] But as Rölvaag's somber trilogy grinds on, the struggle between man and nature, seen with Per Hansa, gives way to the business of human relationships, specifically, the struggle between Peder and Susie, representatives of two strongly opposing cultures. This latter struggle, pervading the third volume, becomes the central fact of the entire trilogy, so that the question is not whether the immigrant pioneer can subdue nature or fate but whether, freed from the past, he can build a society commensurate with his dreams. Here is the test of vaunted American freedom. Peder hopes "to clear the road of a lot of worm-eaten barriers," including, he says in *Peder Victorious,* the "high walls" of racial and cultural prejudice. He hopes that through science, progress, independence of thought, even "through *politics* the Promised Land was to be reached!" Far more than the first-generation immigrant, American-born Peder represents the truly liberated citizen with no heritage save what the frontier instilled. But Peder learns the tragic consequences of striving like Whitman to recreate man and society, of breathing too deeply the air of independence. Ignoring what Santayana once called "the fatal antiquity of human nature,"[14] Peder learns that the conflicting prejudices embodied in both his Norwegian mother and his Irish father-in-law are his and Susie's inheritance too. The frontier experience that both Peder and Susie shared has not reconciled their cultural differences. Instead, Peder's insistence that reconciliation take place only according to what he considers his enlightened common sense drives him to smash Susie's precious crucifix and her vessel for holy water, crunching them viciously beneath his heel, and then to destroy her rosary, bead by bead, grinding them in the same way. Susie cowers horrified by what she witnesses, but Peder, emotionally exhausted after this exercise of personal manifest destiny, sleeps soundly, only to find in the morning Susie's departing note: "Now I've lived the Blessed Day, I've been to the End of the World and have found out what it looks like. I'll never go near there again, because it is an accursed place." At this point the trilogy ends, the name— Peder Victorious—a tragic mockery. One wonders what further mockery Rölvaag intended to depict in still a fourth volume, never written, one which would take Peder to the bloodstained battlefields of World War I where an even greater dream vanished.[15]

III

That this tension between the epic and the tragic, or between *hilder* and the closed wall, supplies the dynamics of the trilogy comes not only from the fact that a similar tension characterized the American frontier myth but that it infused Rölvaag's thinking even before he had emigrated to America. Born and reared on the tiny island of Donna, only five miles from the Arctic Circle, Rölvaag was well acquainted with the unfathomable ways of nature, with the incredible beauty of its summer nights as well as the treachery of its winter storms. In one such storm in 1893 several fishermen from Rölvaag's village drowned, and he himself barely escaped. "That storm," he later wrote, "changed my nature. As the sea broke over us and I believed death was inescapable, I felt a resentment against Destiny."[16] This resentment changed to agonized outrage when in the spring of 1920 his five-year-old son, Paul Gunnar, was drowned while at play. Some eleven years later, three months before his own death, he wrote to his friend, G. F. Newburger: "It's nothing but a common, ordinary, romantic lie that we are the 'captains of our own souls'! Nothing but one of those damned phrases. Just look back over your own life and see how much you have captained! You have been nothing but an ordinary hand in the fo'castle. And that's what we all are."[17]

This brooding note of tragedy, this melancholy and repressed bitterness, darkened Rölvaag's thinking, even while he dedicated nearly twenty-five years of his life to making his own Norwegian people see that to follow an ideal makes them agents in "the creative power of God." Before finishing his undergraduate education he thought of this ideal in terms of *conservation* and *growth*: that true culture in America meant the old must always be preserved in the new. This ideal remained paramount, and even toward the end of his life he spoke of its preservation as "a people's divine creative mission." Yet there was the haunting question that he asked himself again and again: "Must an idealist always die before his thoughts bear fruit?"[18]

What Rölvaag thought to be an American ideal he also interpreted as a personal one. One lesson he learned from his favorite writer, Henrik Ibsen, was that "only as far as the individual can realize himself and all his possibilities will a new society be possible." But from Ibsen he learned another lesson as well. This was the lesson of tragedy, found in *Brand,* namely, that the "free exercise of will . . . results in disaster."[19] It is not surprising that at St. Olaf College Rölvaag's two favorite courses came to be Ibsen's dramas and Norwegian immigration.[20] Nor is it any less surprising that as a boy in Nordland he and his brother Johan, along with two village friends, John and Hans Heitman, read aloud together Kierkegaard's *Either-Or.*[21] Rölvaag was no stranger to ambivalence. The great All or Nothing theme in Ibsen and Kierkegaard is the same tension Rölvaag saw in the immigrants' destiny in America.

Before he polarized this ambivalence in the two characters of Per Hansa and Beret, Rölvaag gave ample hints of the direction he was taking. His first published novel, *Amerika-Breve* (*Letters from America,* 1912), consists of twenty-three letters written by fictional Per Smevik to his father and brother in Norway and collected by the father's friend, Paal Mörck, whose name serves as the novel's pseudonymous author. The letters, based on those Rölvaag wrote home during his early years in South Dakota, thematically juxtapose the new and the old cultures. Per Smevik, who can be called Rölvaag's first Per Hansa figure, strong and ambitious, stands opposite the old-world figure of Mörck whose name means *dark*. Using the same pseudonym, Rölvaag brought bolder strokes to this conflict of cultures in his next novel, *Paa Glemte Veie* (*On Forgotten Paths*, 1914). This novel dramatizes the clash of Chris Larsen, a hard-fighting pioneer who makes a fortune in farming and land speculation, and his physically and temperamentally delicate wife, Magdalene, who stands as Rölvaag's first Beret figure, one who looks longingly to the past. Sympathetic as Rölvaag was to the hardy conqueror of the prairie, this novel makes clear Rölvaag's equally strong feelings for the sensitive, often helpless immigrant who is psychologically unable to cope with frontier life. As for Chris Larsen, who indeed seems able to cope with it, the fact that he survived when his upturned wagon brought death to Magdalene does not blunt the irony that he is later crippled by his runaway horse team and, as an invalid, can only wonder what profit his greed has brought him.

For six years after the publication of *On Forgotten Paths* Rölvaag wrote nothing more significant than textbooks and occasional poems and sketches. But with World War I over, his textbook projects completed, the burgeoning of Norwegian literature with Sigrid Undset, Olav Duun, and Johan Bojer, and, tragically, with the death of his son,[22] Rölvaag snapped out of his lethargy and once again undertook full-length fiction, this time *To Tullinger* (*Two Fools*, 1920), later revised and republished as *Pure Gold* (1930). Once again his theme was greed, though the deeper issue concerned the consequences of cultural rootlessness, the abandoning of the gentler refinements for material opportunities afforded by the New World. This time it is the male character Louis Houglum who harbors respect for tradition, and it is his wife Lizzie who scorns it. Lizzie infects Louis with her avarice, and both these second-generation Norwegian-Americans go the way of Mammon. New traditions replace the old; and the kingdom that the Houglums establish duplicates those Rölvaag saw all around him—Gopher Prairie, Winesburg, Zenith, Spoon River, Tilbury—kingdoms of petty materialism, greed, smugness, and lost souls.

On his more creative levels of vision Rölvaag perceived the gaping disparity between the American dream and the American reality. In his next novel, which immediately precedes the trilogy, he brought to this disparity tightly controlled, artistic handling. This was the novel, more than any other, that Rölvaag considered his favorite. "I have put more of myself into that book than into any other," he once said.[23] Remarking about the book after her husband's death, Jennie Berdahl Rölvaag said he "always felt that it was his own story."[24] Entitled *Laengselens Baat* (*Boat of Longing*, 1921), it was also the immigrant's story, the immigrant in this case with no prairie to conquer but a hostile urban world. Rölvaag once spoke of the story as "the American *Book of Lamentations*,"[25] signifying to him the whole tragic pattern of immigration.

The central point stressed in this novel is that Nils Vaag, the young Norwegian who finds his way to Minneapolis, pays a terrible price for leaving his home in Norway. Not only does he discover that he is out of place because his values conflict with America's materialism, but he also learns the even bigger lesson amid the vulgarity and squalor of the city that his "boat of longing" will never be anything but a Great Northern train taking him to yet another city where, on its busiest corner, he can only stand "searching and searching, like a lone gull perched watchful on some bold headland round which the ocean current runs swift."[26] But this loneliness is more than that of a lost immigrant in an alien city. It is a cleavage of cultures and of generations. Symbolic of this fact is that when Nils's father comes to America to look for him, he gets no further than Ellis Island, where he is told that, because he lacks an affidavit that his son will support him, he must turn back. Old Jo Persa, the father, is then "led through passageway after passageway, out across an open space, down another passage and in through another door, where a key [is] turned on him." There he will wait for *his* "boat of longing," only another crowded steamer taking him away from the new land of his son.

When Rölvaag came to write the trilogy his loyalties wavered between the New World and the Old, between what he often called the "surface" and the "hidden" in American life. It was obvious to him that the nation's official voice proclaimed the former. The platitudes of Theodore Roosevelt in *The Strenuous Life,* published in 1900, boasted of great deeds and great men. And who better than the Captains of Industry represented the fulfillment of the pioneering struggle? Some American writers, however, fixed their attention on the other side of life, even as had some European observers, notably Tocqueville, who predicted that American literature would deal less with surface action and more with passions and ideas. Of course the great nineteenth-century explorers of these dark realms were Poe, Hawthorne, Melville, Twain, and James, all of whom in one way or another recognized the ambivalence in American life but chose to journey where the official voices were never heard. Rölvaag inclined in the same direction, wishing to probe what lay beneath the greatest of all American enterprises.

Rölvaag's great themes in the trilogy were ostensibly to be the Westward Movement and Immigration. These were the subjects that had preoccupied him from the day he first left Norway in 1896, and he had been personally involved in them ever since. But now by Big Island Lake in the northern Minnesota woods where he had built a small cabin, he settled down in the summer of 1922 to undertake that other theme as well, namely, the human cost of these vast American enterprises. What made this deeper, hidden theme important to Rölvaag was again his own ambivalence toward it. Did American success justify the cost? Or, considering the cost, could one say the pioneers had been successful at all? Did the cost nullify the success? Despite the obvious material evidence bespeaking their triumph, did not an irrepressible tragedy darken the full story of the immigrant pioneers?

Physical hardships were one kind of cost. As Parrington noted, Rölvaag was sensitive to the people broken by the frontier, "the great army of derelicts who failed and were laid away . . . in forgotten graves."[27] *Their Fathers' God* opens with the two words "No hope," the stark fact that many settlers no longer had the faith or courage to face repeated crop failure and therefore chose to return to civilization rather than bury their children on the prairie. The scorching heat and the parched, crusted land that Rölvaag describes in this opening scene, and, moreover, the caravans shambling *eastward,* each wagon carrying little more than broken hopes, give evidence that the Myth of the Garden had another side to it. In *Virgin Land* Henry Nash Smith called this other side the "desert," literally the western prairies higher and closer to the Rockies and drier. But the "desert" had its symbolic meaning as well, even amid more fertile land. It was a place of poverty and grinding toil —and of smashed dreams. On the deepest level it was where the immigrant pioneer faced the fact that he was a stranger even among his own people.

To Rölvaag this was the greatest cost of empire building, this loss of a fatherland and of the spiritual associations it nurtured. In Rölvaag's words:

> We came away from our own country and became strangers to our own people. Our pulse can no longer beat in rhythm with the hearts of our own people. We have become strangers—strangers to the people we forsook and strangers to the people we came to. . . . The people we forsook, we remain apart from, and the people we came to, we also remain apart from. We have

thus ceased to be an integral part of a larger whole; we have become something by ourselves, something torn off, without any organic connection either here or there. Herein lies the tragedy of emigration.[28]

This was the tragedy Beret knew best. In the trilogy she is the one who continually measures the achievements of Per Hansa, Peder, and her neighbors against the cost, and she best understands alienation as the essence of that cost. It is not only that her three children come to speak English rather than Norwegian, or even that Peder, the first born in Spring Creek, scoffs at her Norwegian ideas. That she finally becomes a stranger to him suggests still only a portion of the loss she feels. What she essentially loses is her Norwegian soul. This is what America finally demands; this is the price Beret has to pay. Torn loose from her kindred and fatherland, Beret has no place to go; by the time of the second novel "she saw no escape." On sleepless nights she fashions a recurring image:

> She saw herself sitting on a lone rock far out at sea. The surf sucked and boomed. . . . Little by little the surf began sucking her feet. A skua kept circling about the rock. That bird hacked rapaciously at dead bodies floating on the surface—always the eyes. . . . Oh, no, America would not be satisfied with getting their bodies only!

Rölvaag grasped the essential irony in America's promise of freedom and independence. He saw that real freedom and real independence were terrifying prospects because, in their fulfillment, what was demanded was not amalgamation of the old and the new but complete severance. While promising glorious rebirth, the American frontier demanded that the immigrant break all former ties with the past and that here, even in a Garden of Eden, he *must* stay. This was the irony that made Rölvaag's theme especially bitter. The main point in Beret's tragedy is not that she was unable to unite the old and the new; it was that America demanded the sacrifice of the one for the other, and then, after Beret makes the sacrifice, America left her adrift in an alien wilderness where both freedom and independence become a curse.

The American promise is one and the same with its terrible cost. This was Rölvaag's answer to the myth of rebirth and to those other hopes engendered in the American West. Independence meant rootlessness, and from this condition would come spiritual disintegration, regardless of the material prosperity such liberation brings. Disintegration is finally Beret's condition. What Rölvaag leaves us with is an immigrant who has paid the full price. More tragic than Per Hansa, who gives his body to the prairies, Beret gives her Norwegian soul in exchange for nothing more than the prospect that Peder, in his rebellion against the sustaining heritage she herself has sacrificed, will stand strangely alienated from the past, just as she stands apart from the present. This was the tragic cost of independence. Shorn of her interdependencies, Beret could not remake her soul, a transformation Rölvaag said was demanded of every immigrant in the New World. Rebirth, he added, "forever will be beyond the power of the average man," who may give up the old, at the price of spiritual death, but who cannot master the new. On this point Rölvaag was adamant, insisting that the immigrant, "especially the Nordic," cannot uproot himself and move to a new land without paying the ultimate price, the sacrifice of his cultural soul.[29]

It was Rölvaag's passionate idea throughout the trilogy that a people can grow only if they are organically one with their soil and their historical roots. These "hidden" qualities, he thought, supply the spiritual energy by which a transplanted people could sustain their collective aspirations in America. It is for this reason that Beret pleads with her children to speak their native language, to attend their Norwegian Lutheran church, and someday to inspire in their own children the same cultural loyalties she was vainly fighting to retain. She knew that schism spelled both cultural and psychological disaster. Moreover, by the third novel, she knew that people who "turned their backs on their fathers' God were an abomination in the eyes of the Lord." This was her parting admonishment as she lay dying, with both Peder and Susie uncomprehendingly looking on. Her sense of dependency—cultural as well as religious —was what the open frontier spirit demanded she relinquish. That she depended upon a symbolic wall to keep her secure in the knowledge of the past, even in the knowledge of her own sin and in the faith of divine justice, left her a stranger in a land where frontierism repudiated these human dependencies. The trilogy's final chapter ("Father, Forgive Them—!") leaves little doubt as to how Rölvaag resolved the *hilder*-vision that sent this immigrant family to seek a new world on the American horizon.

Even though Rölvaag's sympathies are plainly with Beret and her desolate psychological landscape, it is with Peder that he must finally reckon. Per Hansa's indomitable will and Beret's brooding sense of futility converge in Peder, his birth on Christmas Day, 1873, representing the focal point not only of *Giants,* as Professor Commager suggests, but of the trilogy itself. Commager notes that for Per Hansa the son Peder is "a symbol of victory, for Beret a symbol of sin."[30] This dichotomy recalls the contrast between Per Hansa's swelling optimism, his epic strength and pride, and Beret's guilt. The dichotomy also serves to place Peder firmly between other forces as well. He stands between Per Hansa's quest for the All and Beret's vision of Nothingness. Peder turns away from his mother's preoccupation with the past, but his visionary future, patterned after his father's dreams, carries him no further than the unbending circumstances of the present. Standing between Norwegian Lutheranism and Irish Catholicism, hoping that their convergence will undergird his own Americanism, he yet must live with the fact that *his* own son, whom he and Susie call Petie, was first clandestinely baptized Peder Emmanuel by Beret and Sörine, then later Patrick St. Olaf by Father Williams at Susie's instigation. Other dichotomies clash in Peder, most tellingly in *Their Fathers' God*. Born of the soil and growing to manhood as one who shared the farmers' discontent with Eastern financiers, Peder nevertheless repudiated the Populists' struggle, and in his campaign for District Commissioner in South Dakota he found himself on the side of Republicanism represented by William McKinley and Marcus Hanna. As if this incongruity were not enough, Peder also confronted the shattering accusations of Tom McDougal, his political opponent. In the crowded schoolroom where neighbors for miles around had come to hear the preelection oratory, McDougal mockingly reminded the audience that Peder's dead mother had spent her last months as a "lunatic," that Peder himself was a freethinker who "didn't give two whoops for either God or the devil," and that Peder's wife had had to sneak his son away for secret baptism. Standing helplessly amid these vilifications, which set the new tone of American politics, Peder wanted nothing more than "to vomit." No longer were the issues clear-cut and the political tactics ingenuous. To Peder it seemed that everything America now stood for contradicted the ideals upon which the nation had been built. Like a sudden blast, McDougal's words sent these ideals "whirling around and around." And as if for the first time Peder saw things and heard things he previously would have thought impossible.

It is after this public nightmare that Peder returns home to Susie and in blind rage smashes her crucifix and rosary. Freed at last from these traditional symbols of human dependency, Peder stands alone, with neither wife nor son, with neither religious nor cultural roots. His victory is no less a mockery than his freedom. In the character of Peder Victorious, Rölvaag gave his narrative of immigration and America's westward movement its final tragic significance, echoing in the trilogy's final pages. Like a Greek chorus, Nikoline speaks to Peder of America: "Beautiful . . . and terrible, too." To Peder's question, "terrible in Paradise?" she answers: "There was one standing there, one with a flaming sword. . . . I wasn't allowed to get in!" It is this same tragic lesson that Peder learns.

6

California,
Nathanael West,
and the Journey's End

I

As if by destiny, Walt Whitman's song calling for all
Americans to enlarge their soul harmonized perfectly with
President James K. Polk's intention to enlarge America's
soil. By the time the poet's song was heard, America indeed
had swelled to the Pacific. The achievement following Polk's
inauguration was remarkable: Texas in 1845, the Oregon
Territory in 1848, California in 1850. As counterpoint were
the pulse-tingling words "manifest destiny," handily introduced in 1845 by the editor of the *New York Morning News,*
John L. O'Sullivan, who wrote of "our manifest destiny to
overspread and to possess the whole continent which Providence has given us."[1] By the end of the century this moral

mandate sent Americans seeking still other continents which, perhaps, Providence had also given us. But within this continent alone, the mandate was sufficient reason to allow the United States to fulfill its role as mother of freedom, a role that in the West meant liberating those people suffering under the bondage of England and Mexico. As one Western crusader wrote of the Mexican Californians: "They are only a grade above the aborigines, and like them will be compelled by the very nature of things, to yield to the swelling tide of Anglo-Saxon adventure."[2] The story is, of course, rich in drama; and in looking back over the days of the Oregon and California Trails, the Gold Rush, the railroads, and all those dreamers of the frontier dream, one must agree with Edmund Wilson, who said that California, especially since we took it away from the Mexicans, "had always presented itself to Americans as one of the strangest and most exotic of our adventures."[3]

It would be in California, if at all, where the American frontier dream would be authenticated. Here was the literal end of the trail, and here the Great Promise had to be revealed. Suggestive of this fulfillment is Bayard Taylor's account of the Santa Clara Valley. Commissioned by Horace Greeley to report on the California Gold Rush to the *New-York Tribune,* Taylor wrote that "the unvarying yellow hue of mountain and plain, except where they were transversed by broad belts of dark-green timber, gave a remarkable effect to the view." The mountains especially "seemed to have arrayed themselves in cloth of gold, as if giving testimony to the royal metal which [*sic*] their veins abound."[4] The more prosaic reasons pioneers headed west, and on to California, are well known. Ray Allen Billington uses the term, "abundancy motivation," meaning "a desire to find new pleasures, gratifications, experiences, and achievements."[5] Most of these reasons had to do in some way with economic or social advantage, explained by Frederick Jackson Turner's "safety valve" theory and the mobility enjoyed by those who went west. But there was that other motivation as well, the one that spelled the call of the wild, the unknown, the mystical. California's gold served as the perfect symbol. For his millions of readers Zane Grey's explanation was as good as any: that men in his western land could come "to a supreme proof of the evolution of man, to a realization of God."[6]

To find in California what is strange and exotic is also to discover its tragic groundwork. With desperate effort the frontiersman had crossed the continent; and, decades later, with similar effort, the man from Iowa had saved his money or had planned his career so that, at last, he could go to California to live the good life. As if the continent tilted toward Southern California, the people journeyed to Los Angeles, which, like some vast organism, spread out for miles while its population increased from some fifty thousand in 1890 to over half a million thirty years later. The prospering oil, moving-picture, and aircraft industries were in Los Angeles, but people came also to wrest, sometimes desperately, nothing less than human fulfillment and God's special providence for America. By the 1920s, as one historian says, California had come to be "a sort of middle-class Methodist paradise, with enough sunshine and oranges to give color, enough innovations in the way of airplanes and automobiles and cafeterias to lend excitement, and enough ruggedness—with its jack rabbits and stingarees [stingrays] and hiking trails and surf bathing—to provide adventure."[7] For the non-Methodists, life in Los Angeles promised to be "one long cocktail of orange blossoms, ocean beaches, and Spring Street."[8] Intent upon creating an exotic Mediterranean culture, enthusiasts named their towns Arcadia, Hesperia, Morocco, Verona; Abbot Kinney spent a fortune developing "Venice," a cultural center near Pasadena replete with canals, weeping willow trees, gondolas, singing gondoliers, and imported Venetian pigeons; and with the help of Henry Huntington and others, Frank Miller of Riverside built Mission Inn, called "the Alhambra" of the Pacific Coast by its many renowned visitors who sat quietly in the shade of lemon trees and bougainvillea to listen to mission bells.

All these efforts to create a paradise where dreams come true, where health is restored, physically and spiritually, after one's long years on the severe Nebraska or Dakota prairie, and where fullness of life has something to do with exotic surroundings—these efforts kept pace with the flow of newcomers. Los Angeles became the mecca for cultists of all description—"sick survivors of New England transcendentalism," said Paul Jordan-Smith, a long-time Los Angeles spokesman who, in an essay entitled "Los Angeles: Ballyhooers in Heaven," noted that the milder climate enabled them "to keep the illusion that they have conquered disease through spiritual power."[9] During the 1920s the "religious awakening" in Los Angeles reached such proportions that legislation finally forced soothsayers, fortune-tellers, and swamis to operate under license. As the oasis for divine healing, occult science, reincarnation, and astrological revelations, the city in 1926 had seven separate churches of the American Theosophical Society and twenty-one of the National Spiritualist Association.[10] Living in palaces of opulent optimism or surging along Spring Street, the people seized at whatever offered uplift, be it the faith of some newly arrived prophet or only another pamphlet announcing still another real estate subdivision, this one perhaps named Eve's Garden. As Paul Jordan-Smith observed, Los Angeles was "less a city of angels than a paradise of realtors and a refuge for the rheumatics." The point, as he notes, is that the newcomers hoped to find their Promised Land in Los Angeles, their "American Port Said," and instead discovered "a population of Iowa farmers and sunburned old maids in an endless chain of cafeterias, movie palaces and state picnics"—in short, the city of angels was "just as dull as the traditional kingdom of heaven."[11]

Wherein is the tragedy? Simply and profoundly in the disparity between illusion and reality, between the promise and its nullification. In the American Westward Movement, California came to symbolize the logical conclusion of America itself. Not only had a continent been crossed, but in the West lived a new breed (some thought even to call them a new species, endowed, said P. D. Ouspensky, Annie Besant, and others, with "higher consciousness") that had sloughed off the past with its stale traditions and built a civilization more uniquely American than anything in the Ohio Valley or the Virginia Piedmont. But if at the trail's end there was only fool's gold, if fulfillment failed to square with expectation, if with unabated frenzy Californians were *still* seeking their Promised Land, then what follows must be despair, first mute, then violent, according to the extent of hope originally proffered. It is this scene of the American Westerner with nowhere left to go, with the frontier closed, with only California at his feet, with shore and waves but no "passage to India," that the pioneer never dared to imagine. The one dream he dared not dream was now exactly the one he did not need to dream, for he now confronted the reality that his transcendental self, which had previously been supported by the metaphor of the open frontier, no longer found a safety valve through which to escape. Space had closed in upon him.

It was not merely that he had to readjust to a closed-space existence in the literal sense. Living in cities rather than on prairies, accepting more governmental restriction, getting along within complex communication and transportation systems, coping with automation, or adjusting to a thousand other situations unique to twentieth-century urban America have little to do with what it means to face the closed frontier as a metaphor of tragedy, except as these situations reinforce the metaphor. Nor was it that the Westerner had not asked the fateful question about existence. It was instead that he had not asked it in terms of his *own* existence. It became obvious, after his finding California something less than what the rainbow promised, that he still would not force questions upon existence interpreted as tragedy. He would rather manufacture the dreamworld he desperately sought, or else he would destroy his dream factories, his fellow spirits, and himself in one apocalyptic holocaust.

II

If it is legitimate to trace the Westward Movement to its logical end in California, and if the whole incremental symbolism of this movement can be given a California setting, then the work of Nathanael West must be read as a profound interpretation of how the great myth of the West comes to an end. Writers of greater stature than West have written about California. One immediately thinks of F. Scott Fitzgerald and John Steinbeck, or such satirists as Aldous Huxley and Evelyn Waugh. One also thinks of all those writers who spent their last years in Southern California: Julian Hawthorne in Pasadena; Hamlin Garland and Theodore Dreiser, who found Hollywood culture perfect for their spiritualistic pursuits; a potpourri of other writers including Upton Sinclair, Edgar Rice Burroughs, Gene Stratton Porter, Rupert Hughes, and Zane Grey; and a handful of foreign authors including Huxley, Franz Werfel, and, for a time, Thomas Mann. Yet, strangely enough, Nathanael West was like none of these, just as his *The Day of the Locust* (1939) brings the frontier to a tragic close as does no other American novel.

The critical attention West has received since 1950, ten years after his death in California, makes clear that his works—especially *Miss Lonelyhearts* (1933) and *The Day of the Locust*—have found an important place in American literature. As perceptive a critic as Stanley Edgar Hyman, for example, considers *Miss Lonelyhearts* "one of the three finest novels of our century. The other two," he says, "are F. Scott Fitzgerald's *The Great Gatsby* and Ernest Hemingway's *The Sun Also Rises.*"[12] This judgment is patently extreme, since it excludes William Faulkner, to mention only one name. But Hyman's assertion does take one squarely to the fact that Nathanael West deserves a careful reading, one that reveals in him the tragic awareness that life and death are interwoven, that the West is both a place to live and a place to die. It is, in fact, this tragic perspective that gives his novels such compelling importance to the person who finds an ineluctable tragedy in American frontierism.

This is not to say that West's writing is restricted to this American theme, nor is it to place him among only American writers of his own day. James F. Light suggests strong resemblances between West and Dostoevsky; Angel Flores sees West as living in the haunted castles of Salvador Dali and Giorgio di Chirico; Victor Comerchero finds echoes of T. S. Eliot's *The Waste Land* nearly everywhere in West; and, in his writing of *Miss Lonelyhearts,* West himself acknowledges indebtedness to William James, John Bunyan, and Leo Tolstoy.[13] It is to argue strongly, however, that Nathanael West has contributed to an American view of tragedy and that, as this view relates to the dominant metaphor of the closed frontier, his position in American literature grows ever stronger. Even in his independence, his work reflects interesting similarities to that of Sherwood Anderson and F. Scott Fitzgerald. Randall Reid, for example, gives considerable attention to the way *The Day of the*

Locust and *Winesburg, Ohio* are alike. Like Homer Simpson in West's novel, Anderson's characters long to return to Eden, which "beckons somewhere in the distance." But at the moment of release—defined as "expressive communion with someone else"—they are irrevocably thwarted, and the tragic fact is that in both Anderson and West, "the grotesque is normal."[14] As for West and Fitzgerald, one discovers many similarities as well as the uncanny coincidence that the two writers died only a few miles apart on successive days. Both men came from American fringe groups, one Jewish and the other Irish Catholic; both went to Paris after college; both created unforgettable images of the waste land, one of old movie lots and the other of the Valley of Ashes; both wrote "last" novels about Hollywood; both, observes David D. Galloway, had "an agonized sense of the ironies of life, and their heroes all embarked on the fatal race for a green light or a silver screen image that continually receded before them"[15]; and, according to Edmund Wilson, both failed "to get the best out of their best years" because, in part at least, they succumbed to Hollywood "with its already appalling record of talent depraved and wasted."[16]

Instead of succumbing to Hollywood, West found there the instant symbol for the theme he had been developing ever since his first novel, *The Dream Life of Balso Snell* (1931). The same relationship with Hollywood obtains in his style, which takes on the kind of radical distortion he later found pervading life in Southern California. Far more than either Anderson or Fitzgerald, West artistically wove something monstrous and misshapen into his novels, the same qualities the French surrealists brought to their work. Like them West recreated a twisted, demented world. It is true he did this before he saw Hollywood, for even in his first two books, *Balso Snell* and *Miss Lonelyhearts,* this kind of bizarre world exists. But his trip to Hollywood in 1933 and his return for good in 1935 confirmed the American correlative. His third novel, *A Cool Million* (1934), demolishes the American Horatio Alger myth, and *The Day of the Locust* does the same to the frontier myth. In both style and theme this novel culminates his work, despite what one might speculate about later novels, had he survived the automobile accident on December 22, 1940, when he was only thirty-seven years old. For in *The Day of the Locust* West uses Hollywood as the locus for his tragic theme. Or, put differently, in Hollywood West transmogrifies this theme into something uniquely American.

III

Balso Snell was published the same year (1931) Nathanael West legally changed his name from Nathan Weinstein, although he had written the novel six years earlier when he was living in Paris. Considering that he was only twenty-two at the time, it is remarkable that this first novel should have contained, as Comerchero correctly observes, "the key to all his later works."[17] It is equally striking that he chose the name he did for himself. When questioned about this, West answered, "Horace Greeley said, 'Go West, young man.' So I did."[18] Light notes that since West was always careful in choosing names for his fictional characters, he could not have missed what his own new name implied. As an explicit metaphor in his last novel, it also announces the theme found in all four novels and introduced in *Balso Snell* with the opening epigram: "After all, my dear fellow, life, Anaxagoras has said, is a journey."[19] What Comerchero surprisingly gives only cursory attention to is that in this "key" novel West is preoccupied with the tragic nature of that journey.

The journey Balso takes seems little more than an

outrageous parody. After entering the "mystic portal," ("O Anus Mirabilis!") of the Greeks' famous wooden horse, Balso sees "a beautiful Doric prostate gland"; he enters "the large intestine" and, while talking with his guide about art as "sublime excrement," makes headway "up the tube." Down "the great tunnel" he comes upon Maloney the Areopagite who, "naked except for a derby in which thorns were sticking," was trying "to crucify himself with thumb tacks." After listening to Maloney's biography of Saint Puce, a flea who lived in the armpit of Christ, Balso turns "a bend in the intestine" and encounters a boy with a diary supposedly written for his teacher, Miss McGeeney. The entries are mostly his "Crime Journal," one signed "John Raskolnikov Gilson" and another containing the boy's long Dostoevskian dreamlike account of how he murdered an idiot neighbor. Putting the diary aside, Balso takes up a pamphlet, again supposedly written by Miss McGeeney's young student, who reflects upon the death of Saniette, a smart and sophisticated woman representing the type of audience for whom he, the youthful student, writer, and actor, sees himself as "a tragic clown," one who must "burlesque the mystery of feeling at its source" and then "laugh at the laugh." Balso next spies Miss McGeeney herself—"a middle aged woman dressed in a mannish suit and wearing hornrimmed glasses"—who succeeds in grabbing Balso and forcing him to listen to her new biography, *Samuel Perkins: Smeller.* He finally frees himself, hits her "a terrific blow in the gut," throws her into a fountain, and then wonders if the only people inhabiting the wooden horse are "writers in search of an audience." He next encounters Janey Davenport, called "the Lepi," a hunchback with a "beautiful, hydrocephalic forehead," who agrees to "yield" to Balso after he first kills her lover, Beagle Darwin. Nothing comes from this arrangement except that Balso reads two letters Beagle wrote to Janey explaining that he, Beagle, refused to take her to Paris because he was convinced the trip would result in her suicide. Actually the letters recapitulate her hypothetical suicide and Beagle's feigned madness following it. At this point in his journey Balso "awoke" and now sees Miss McGeeney, who explains that she wrote the two letters as part of a novel. She identifies herself as Mary, Balso's old friend. They make love, his ejaculation being nothing more than a wet dream as the novel ends.

Fantastic parody that this novel is, West is deadly serious about the subjects he treats. There is no mistaking his indictment against art and the patronizing art-lovers over whose heads, he says at one point, the ceiling of the theater ought to be made to open and "cover the occupants with tons of loose excrement." His position against church and culture, especially the commercialization of both, is equally petulant. All that "Home and Duty, Love and Art" represents comes under scathing parody, sustained throughout by what Balso Snell's initials clearly stand for. But on a deeper level West condemns whatever gets in the way of honest feeling. Here is his castigation of literature, if what one knows about "Death, Love, Beauty" or "Love, Life, Death" consists merely of words that protect one from experience. Equally intolerable as protection against reality is philosophic idealism, which reconciles the Plural into the Singular, does away with beginnings and ends, and appropriates the circle as its illusory symbol of human existence. Such monism, Balso reads in the pamphlet, is like Saniette's "hiding under the blankets of her hospital bed and invoking the aid of Mother Eddy . . . ; 'I won't die! I'm getting better and better. I won't die.' " In the same way Beagle Darwin speculates about ways to avoid the fact of death as he imagines Janey Davenport's suicide. His alternatives are to remain "cold, calm, collected, almost stolid"; to stay in his ivory tower of thought and refuse to disturb "that brooding white bird, my spirit"; to call himself the "Buffoon of the

New Eternities" and, like Mary Baker Eddy, preach that life is merely "the absence of Death" and Death merely "the absence of Life"; or to feign either sadness or madness. In short, like a tragic clown, to "convert everything into fantastic entertainment" (parody), finally laughing at the laugh itself.

At the heart of the novel is Dante's dark wood, described in the pamphlet and the two letters Balso reads. Here is where Balso's journey takes him. "It seems to me," he reads in the pamphlet, "as though all the materials of life —wood, glass, wool, skin—are rubbing against my sty, my cold sore and my pimples; rubbing in such a way as not to satisfy the itch or convert irritation into active pain, but so as to increase the size of the irritation, magnify it and make it seem to cover everything—hysteria, despair." For this condition, for this irritation of the spirit, there is neither relief nor escape: neither Keats, music, mathematics, nor architecture. This tragic condition is not to be surmounted or transcended. No mystic revelation will come either to justify or to annul it. Only by playing the clown can one cope with it. And, asks Beagle Darwin, "What is more tragic than the role of clown?" The clown pretends the illusions are real, but he knows that "Life is but the span from womb to tomb; a sigh, a smile; a chill, a fever; a throe of pain, a spasm of volupty [*sic*]: then a gasping for breath, and the comedy is over, the song is ended, ring down the curtain, the clown is dead."

The novel depicts the tragedy of man, whose birth is signaled not by the Three Kings, the Dove, or the Star of Bethlehem, but only by "old Doctor Haasenschweitz who wore rubber gloves and carried a towel over his arm like a waiter." "The tragedy of all of us" is that we are only human, that our father came not as the mythical swan, bull, or shower of gold; he came only from the bathroom and "with his pants unsupported by braces." We were conceived, not like Christ, Dionysus, or Gargantua, but like the deformed Janey Davenport—"in an offhand manner on a rainy afternoon."

The crucial ambiguity of the novel is whether or not Balso understands what he has read in the pamphlet and in Beagle Darwin's two letters. Does he know where his journey has taken him, and does he discover what it means for man to play the role of tragic clown? It seems clear that Balso's mystical experience at the end of the novel when the "Two became One," paralleling the moment when he and Mary McGeeney copulate, can only be West's parodical coup de grace suggesting something more closely akin to Sartre's horrible ecstasy. If, then, Balso Snell's dreamworld is one of total delusion, if what he takes as a miracle is only hysteria and despair, then the ambiguity perfectly serves the novel's irony, namely, that Balso Snell journeys to what for him is meaningless. His journey to the tragic depths brings him nothing more than the grandest of all illusions —his "shout of triumph . . . victorious, relieved."

More than Balso, Miss Lonelyhearts, in West's next novel, understands that life is a "stinking business." To those who endure it because they are either too witless or, like Melville's Bartleby, too honest to run from it, Miss Lonelyhearts compassionately murmurs, "Ah, humanity." But in his public statements, printed as advice in his newspaper lovelorn column, Miss Lonelyhearts offers much more. To Sick-of-it-all and Desperate and Broken-hearted and Disillusioned-with-tubercular-husband he writes that "Life *is* worth while, for it is full of dreams and peace, gentleness and ecstasy, and faith that burns like a clear white flame on a grim dark altar." At the same time he knows his words fail to meet the exigencies of those persons who seek his help. The words also fail to assuage his own life of quiet desperation. Miss Lonelyhearts' journey is a via dolorosa, a forbidding effort to undergird promises with facts. "Christ is love" is the promise; the letters heaped on his desk each day are the facts. An abyss lies between.

If only Miss Lonelyhearts himself could believe the promise, "then everything would be simple and the letters extremely easy to answer." But he is caught in the condition of one to whom knowledge and belief are vastly disparate. Various escapes beguile him from this trap: nature, the South Seas, hedonism, art, sex, humanism, marriage and home, even drugs and suicide. Each offers some reconciliation; each answers some of his questions. Instead of peace, however, they only leave him with a strange exhaustion, yet with a desperate compulsion to continue seeking, even though no signs of spring, no "target" in the sky, offer hope.

What makes Miss Lonelyhearts a tragic figure is that in a belittered world he seeks order, Christian order founded on Christ's love. "If you love everything," Miss Lonelyhearts reads in *The Brothers Karamazov,* "you will perceive the divine mystery in things. . . . And you will come at last to love the whole world with an all-embracing love." These words spoken by Father Zossima to Alyosha were now taken by Miss Lonelyhearts into the Dismal Swamp, where he had a vision of the world as a great pawnshop and of himself as one who was appointed to set its litter aright. All the fur coats, diamong rings, watches, shotguns, fishing tackle, mandolins—all this "paraphernalia of suffering"— Miss Lonelyhearts attacked, first arranging everything into a giant phallus, then a diamond, and after these a circle, triangle, square, swastika. Not until he fashioned a gigantic cross was his vision complete. Each shape symbolized a *Weltanschauung.* The cross symbolized his own. His decision to act upon this Christ-dream, to reconcile his actions with the Christ-promise, is the desperate wager. "He had played with this thing ['this Christ business'], but had never allowed it to come alive." His gamble is to battle the world's chaos with love.

This gamble is like the turning point of Melville's novel *Pierre,* when Pierre throws himself upon the Chronometrical instead of the Horological. To Pierre chronometrical standards come to represent "ideas celestial" whereas the horological ones represent "things terrestrial." The analogy with time is that while a Greenwich chronometer indicates twelve o'clock high noon, local watches elsewhere will indicate a different time, say, twelve o'clock midnight. Melville says the former "will always" contradict the latter. Thus heavenly wisdom, analogous with chronometrical or absolute time, is earthly folly. Melville explains that, for the mass of men, heavenly or chronometrical righteousness "is not only impossible, but would be entirely out of place, and positively wrong" in our horological, everyday, and relative world. Christ's injunction, for example, that when struck on one cheek we turn the other is chronometrical: so also his injunction that we give *all* we have to the poor. In short, the chronometrical and horological conceit teaches that "in things terrestrial (horological) a man must not be governed by ideas celestial (chronometrical)."[20] If he is, Christ's crucifixion makes clear the consequence.

In *Miss Lonelyhearts* Shrike embodies the horological. With terrifying insight he knows the folly of Miss Lonelyhearts' living in this world by the standards of the other. But like Pierre, Miss Lonelyhearts crosses the Rubicon and gambles on the chronometrical. He admits to a "Christ complex," and even though his friends mockingly call him a "leper licker," he declares himself a "humanity lover." In the novel's final chapter, entitled "Miss Lonelyhearts Has a Religious Experience," a mystic vision comes to him as he stares at a figure of Christ hung on his bedroom wall. He sees that the real Christ is "life and light." For a moment his room is "full of grace," his identification with God "complete." He has seen Christian order; his pawnshop world fits together into a beautiful Oneness and he with it.

But like the fateful knocking on the gate in *Macbeth,* a doorbell shatters the vision of Miss Lonelyhearts, who goes to the top of the stairs to watch Peter Doyle, a cripple, trudging up toward him. Fresh from his religious experience, Miss Lonelyhearts takes Doyle for another Desperate, Broken-hearted, Sick-of-it-all, and rushes to embrace him with love. A bullet from the gun of Doyle, who had his own grievances against Miss Lonelyhearts, sends the deluded savior tumbling down the stairs, down into the very horological world he thought he could transform. Christian love has been shattered by life.

At the end of their respective journeys both Balso Snell and Miss Lonelyhearts supposedly experience a mystical Oneness with all things. As if absorbed in God and made God, Balso merges with "the One that is all things and yet no one of them" and Miss Lonelyhearts experiences "two rhythms that were slowly becoming one. . . . His heart was the one heart, the heart of God." But nothing in West could be more ironic. Balso's expanded consciousness was only sexual fantasy and Miss Lonelyhearts' Truth only the stage setting for the real truth, namely, that life is violence, not love.

In two separate articles Thomas M. Lorch strenuously argues that Miss Lonelyhearts is a religious saint: he first withdraws from the world in order to correct it, he subdues selfhood, he undergoes a dark night of the soul, and then he finally knows the joy of mystical union with God.[21] To support this interpretation, Lorch cites West's statement, found in a short piece he entitled "Some Notes on Miss L.," that "Miss Lonelyhearts became the portrait of a priest of our time who has a religious experience."[22] It must be noted, however, that in the novel Shrike corrosively makes an almost identical observation: "Did I myself not say that the Miss Lonelyhearts are the priests of twentieth-century America?" That Shrike jokes at the hollowness of such priesthood is not too different from the way Nathanael West mockingly brings each of his protagonist's journeys to a dead-end. With Miss Lonelyhearts and Lemuel Pitkin in *A Cool Million* West is audaciously ironic by bestowing martyrdom on them. ("He [Miss Lonelyhearts] smiled at Shrike as the saints are supposed to have smiled at those about to martyr them.") Rather than showing Miss Lonelyhearts as a religious saint—one, says Lorch, whose "positive religious development is toward Christ-like love and sacrifice, and from doubt to faith"[23]—West shows the tragic grotesqueness of this development. Thinking himself another Christ, Miss Lonelyhearts rushes to make the cripple, Peter Doyle, "whole again," but instead, the savior, felled by the bullet, drags the cripple down with him in a crazy reversal of the resurrection. His mystical union with God and his vision of himself as a savior could hardly be more ironic, unless the role of tragic clown be played by Lemuel Pitkin, another crippled martyr, whose last words before an assassin's bullet found *its* mark were: "I am a clown . . . but there are times when even clowns must grow serious. This is such a time. I. . . ."

IV

In his third novel, *A Cool Million,* written after his 1933 visit to Hollywood, West sends his deluded protagonist, Lemuel Pitkin, on a journey that literally costs him his teeth, an eye, a thumb, his scalp, a leg, and finally his life. Comic as this business is, the underlying seriousness concerns West's devastating treatment of American capitalism and his complete renunciation of the frontier myth. Out to seek his fortune like a western Horatio Alger, Lemuel encounters frauds and con men of every description, each carrying out the great American prerogative of free enterprise. Deluded by the notion that others are as innocently engaged as himself, Lemuel goes his way, incredulously finding himself in one dead-end after another. The biggest fraud of all is Nathan "Shagpoke" Whipple, former president of the United States as well as of the Rat River National Bank. It is with "Shagpoke" that the guileless Lemuel goes to California to dig gold, an outrageous adventure that leaves Lemuel without his scalp and a leg; and it is also with him that Lemuel travels "many weary months" as the chief attraction of their tent show, in which Lemuel, showing off his scalped skull, is hailed as the only survivor of the Yuba River massacre. For a while the two adventurers—one as guileless as the other is cunning—work for S. Snodgrasse's road show, which features the "Chamber of American Horrors / Animate and Inanimate / Hideosities." With a gigantic, electrically lighted hemorrhoid in the center, the "inanimate" exhibit displays objects "whose distinction lay in the great skill with which their materials had been disguised": paper made to look like wood, "wood like rubber, rubber like steel, steel like cheese, cheese like glass, and, finally, glass like paper . . . pencil sharpeners that could also be used as earpicks, can openers as hair brushes . . . flower pots that were really victrolas, revolvers that held candy, candy that held collar buttons and so forth." The "animate" part of the show is a pageant showing Quakers "being branded, Indians brutalized and cheated, Negroes sold, children sweated to death." Culminating the pageant is a playlet set first in "a typical American home" where a white-haired grandmother is hoodwinked out of her money by a "sleek salesman," and then on a busy street where the grandmother and her three starved grandchildren lie dead while two laughing millionaires, almost tripping over the corpses, curse "the street cleaning department for its negligence."

Duped, defrauded, and literally decimated, Lemuel is

still not shaken by what has clearly become an American nightmare, complete with West's masterful surrealism. Lemuel, whose grotesque disfigurement shockingly contrasts with his innocence, continues to believe in the American Dream, which West shows as defrauding all Americans who, holding desperately to it, go to California to have it come true. Calling on the "Golden Gates Employment Bureau," Lemuel gratefully takes a job as stooge in still another road show, this one featuring a Riley-Robbins team who in the last act bring out an enormous wooden mallet called "The Works" and proceed to "demolish" him. First his toupee flies off, then his glass eye and false teeth pop out, and finally his wooden leg is knocked into the audience which, at this point, is "convulsed with joy."

In this novel West is working toward the kind of mob violence marking certain scenes in *Huckleberry Finn*. But with West this violence more sharply reflects what Daniel Aaron has called the "fascist mentality" of a people "ripe for catastrophe."[24] These are the people justified by the illusion of their own innocent righteousness. The more fanatically they defend the illusion, the more violently and joyfully they make victims of those who, by their existence alone, vex it. This fanaticism coupled with a suspicion that they themselves are victims of some gigantic fraud brings on the totally destructive riot marking the end of what Nathanael West envisioned for the American frontier journey. The sweeping, engulfing violence in West's last novel is only incipient in *A Cool Million*. But its terror is nonetheless real, as seen not only in Lemuel's disfigurement but in the riot "Shagpoke" incited in the name of his fascist National Revolutionary Party, a riot in which southern white Protestant citizens of Beulah raise the Confederate flag on their courthouse staff and then proceed to parade the heads of Negroes on poles, nail a Jew to the door of his hotel room, and rape the local Catholic priest's housekeeper.

Unlike Huck Finn, Lemuel has nowhere "to light out" to. Illusory as Huck's escape was, Lemuel's open frontier is an even greater illusion. For Lemuel the frontier was closed even before he started his journey, and his innocence could never survive, let alone be reborn. In Huck's world there was still nature, and there was love between him and Jim. In Lemuel's world neither exists. There is only the chaos of violence, brutality, fanaticism, and dissemblance, a closed world in which nature is synthetic and people are hell. The great difference between Huck and Lemuel is that whereas Huck recognized evil for what it was, Lemuel perceives nothing beyond his dreamworld. Huck's innocence felt the crush of reality. Lemuel's innocence, on the other hand, feels nothing, even though he is literally torn apart by the real world. Actually Lemuel's is not innocence at all but a parody of it. Nothing tragic marks Lemuel as a character because he realizes nothing about either himself or his world. Thoroughly duped and deceived he dies a martyr for a cause he neither understands nor upholds. He dies a spokesman for the same forces of destruction that hail him as a martyr, the same forces that are intent upon making America "again American," the kind of fascism that will *have* its American Dream, come fire or brimstone.

That Lemuel Pitkin is not a tragic figure does not mean that West suspended his tragic view in *A Cool Million*. Even though West never created a character of fully tragic dimensions, he did portray what can be called a tragic society. It is also true that he depicted certain characters whose dreams led to tragic consequences. Especially with Miss Lonelyhearts, these consequences are psychologically and spiritually credible. But West's creative insights focus more sharply upon masses than upon individuals. His concern is what happens to a society whose collective dream contradicts reality, whose only way of confronting a closed frontier is by dreaming it is still open. This is why his tragic insights are peculiarly American. As early as his first novel and his reference in it to Mary Baker Eddy, West identified the society as American, and in his next novel he refers to Miss Lonelyhearts as representative of "the priests of twentieth-century America." The society is unmistakably American in *A Cool Million,* and by the time he wrote *The Day of the Locust* West concentrates all his vitriol upon a single place, Hollywood, and upon a single dream, the frontier. West's cynicism, anger, mockery, and disgust cover the general malaise of modern man, but it is to the twentieth-century American that he brings his full creative attention. Even though his earlier three novels have their own artistic integrity, they serve, nevertheless, as a long prelude to his final masterpiece. All that is in the earlier novels is to be found in *The Day of the Locust,* and the powerful concentration is well-nigh overwhelming. No angrier book in American literature has been written since *The Confidence-Man* and *The Mysterious Stranger.* And few American novels can surpass it for what it depicts as the American tragedy.

V

An inevitableness distinguishes West's last novel, as if by fate it was indeed to be his final work. In it the assumptions of the earlier works are not only elaborated, as V. L. Lokke suggests,[25] but they carry eschatological importance. The masses in *The Day of the Locust* are waiting for the end. They dream with latent "messianic rage" of the last big miracle. No longer are they individually tragic clowns like Abe Kusich and Harry Greener or even little Adore. They are now the "locust" with "wild, disordered minds" and "awful, anarchic power" to destroy civilization. They are the cultists and mad dreamers, standing before their New Thought shrines and awaiting the revelation that the

Golden West promised. The sex-dream, the Christ-dream, the million-dollar-dream—all tried and untrue—must now make way for the paradise-dream: "Why," says Maybelle Loomis, an old-time Westerner of six years, California is "a paradise on earth."

Like Harry Greener who once restricted his clowning to the stage but who now clowns continuously as "his sole method of defense," the hordes dare not see Hollywood for the dream dump it is. To do so would be, as Lemuel Pitkin discovered, to "grow serious," and at such a moment reality crashes in. In West's novel society has become clownlike—for example, the fat lady in the yachting cap who was going shopping, not boating; or the man in the Tyrolean hat who was returning from an insurance office, not a mountain. Hollywood, once a stage, is now a way of life, a paradise for masqueraders.

Something inevitable was in West's choice of Hollywood as the setting for this novel. As Aaron points out, West does not merely give a "superficial arraignment of the film colony," nor does he intend "a romantic evocation of Hollywood as epic," after the manner of Evelyn Waugh or F. Scott Fitzgerald. Instead, says Aaron, Hollywood is a "symbol of despair and unfulfillment."[26] Even more to the point, it symbolizes the fateful destiny of a society living on illusions rather than facing existence as tragedy.

There is also a terrible inevitability in what Tod Hackett will paint. Hired to learn set and costume designing, Tod left the Yale School of Fine Arts to go west. It is through his eyes we see the people whom Tod felt he had to paint. About them he at first knew very little except that "they had come to California to die." But as this "very complicated young man" wanders amid the sets and costumes of the real Hollywood, the painting takes shape in his mind. Each fragment, a little more terrifying than the last, falls into place. As prophet-artist he plans "The Burning of Los Angeles" to show the flames like "bright flags." Los Angeles will have a "gala air" as it burns. The people who set it on fire will be a "holiday crowd." As prophet he sees more than a single city gone mad. Angelenos may be the "cream" of America's madmen, and their city may be the first to be consumed in flame, but "their comrades all over the country would follow. There would be civil war." Amid a screaming tidal wave of humanity—a crowd turned "demoniac"—Tod imagines what his painting will show when finished. The holocaust will be what it has already become. His vision becomes the fact; his dream of doom, the doom itself. Tod, who from the first made every effort to remain detached and objective, is broken in both body and mind. With a fractured leg he is lifted into a police car, its siren only a little louder than his own hysterical scream.

West said that this novel showed "the peculiar half-world" of Hollywood.[27] Reid speculates that the force in this half-world resembles a Freudian "revolt of a mass id against those 'higher' powers which have denied it and tricked it"; or a Marxian "outrage of victims who have been cynically exploited by a system"; or a Nietzschean "revenge of Dionysian frenzy against a fraudulent Apollonian dream."[28] More striking than these suggestions is what D. H. Lawrence called the "inner diabolism" below the surface of American life or what Melville called the "power of blackness." It is a power only the greatest American writers have probed. It is a power of tragedy, that fateful nemesis which to prove its agency destroys the dreamer.

West shows a power of violence beneath Hollywood's facade, a surging force not to be placated by swimming pools, fast cars, and movie premieres, and emphatically not by Hollywood's bizarre churches, such as "The Church of Christ, Physical" or the "Tabernacle of the Third Coming" or the "Temple Moderne." Throughout all West's novels this ominous force lies under the surface, sometimes breaking out in Balso's dream of murder; in *Miss Lonelyhearts* it may be the violence accompanying the sacrament, or stories of gang rape, or Miss Lonelyhearts' own violence against the old man sitting on the toilet cover who refused to tell his life story like another Broken-hearted or Sick-of-it-all. American success-at-any-price accounts for much of the violence in *A Cool Million*. In *The Day of the Locust* violence and prophecies of violence shatter nearly every scene. In a short piece entitled "Some Notes on Violence," written in 1932 when he joined William Carlos Williams in editing the little magazine *Contact*, West observed that "almost every manuscript we receive has violence for its core." The manuscripts came "from every state in the Union, from every type of environment, yet their highest common denominator is violence." "In America," West said, "violence is idiomatic."[29] In his own novels there is that peculiarly American penchant for what in *Miss Lonelyhearts* West calls an "orgy of stone breaking." Beneath the physical acts of violence West probes for causes that, it becomes evident in *The Day of the Locust*, pertain to the fact that Americans have smashed their cultural heritage. Rather than merely sloughing off their Old-World traditions, they have rebelled against them, they have smashed them, much in the manner of Rölvaag's Peder Victorious. With desperation they seek a new order, for, as Frederick J. Hoffman observes in *The Mortal No*, "man is above all a formalizing creature, and his sanity and balance depend upon the success of his comprehending experience formally."[30]

The new order is the frontier and, inevitably, Southern California. As with Miss Lonelyhearts, who developed "an almost insane sensitiveness to order," the American who saved his dollars and rejected his heritage journeyed west to the land of sunshine and oranges, accepting the desperate wager to unite with this order celebrated by mystics like Whitman and cultists like Maybelle Loomis, the "rawfoodist" and follower of Dr. Pierce, whose motto was "Know-All Pierce-All."

One such American in West's last novel is Homer Simpson, whom Tod immediately recognized as "an exact model" for the westward-bound. Homer had worked for twenty years as a hotel bookkeeper in Wayneville, Iowa; he had saved his money; he had gone to California for his health. Reading West's summation of Homer's forty years in Iowa is like encountering Tolstoy's Ivan Ilych, whose life had been simple, ordinary, and "therefore terrible." Homer's forty years had been "without variety or excitement," a life of "totaling figures and making entries." Vulnerable as he is to the Hollywood dream befitting his name, Homer instead is stunned by the crazy, violent half-world represented especially by Harry Greener and his daughter Faye. Moreover, he confronts his own emptiness, his constantly trembling hands signaling the existential panic he feels within himself. Knowing his "anguish is basic," he thinks of yet other frontiers—of Mexico "only a few hundred miles away" or of the boats leaving daily for Hawaii. Unlike Faye, who has the wild energy for violence, and unlike Harry Greener, who can laugh a horrible, "machinelike screech," Homer can only cry and, in the end, coil foetus-like on his bed, an escape far better, thinks Tod, than Religion, Art, or the South Sea Islands.

Homer's "Uterine Flight" as an alternative to the acceptance of life as tragedy contrasts with that other alternative, violence. Both lead to self-destruction, but it is the destruction of society that preoccupies West, the kind of anarchic energy that impels the mob to have its own blood. Having dreamed the great dream and found it fraudulent, having gone to California and found even the sun a joke, the people feed on violence. With nothing else to titillate their ennui, they devour the newspapers and movies, the endless suppliers of sex crimes, explosions, murder, and war. Yet this fare is not sufficient, for theirs is a deeper sickness than boredom. Not only do they feel cheated but, more importantly, they feel lost. They no longer know who or where they are, so successful has been their masquerading and so monstrous are their phony Swiss chalets, Mediterranean villas, Egyptian temples, and Mexican ranch houses. Their anonymity breeds fear and their fear, hate. These are the dark powers too voracious to be satisfied by cock fights or a staged Waterloo.

The final scene of the novel is like nothing else in American literature, unless it be Hawthorne's "Earth's Holocaust," a story set on the western prairie, where a giant fire consumes the vestigial remains of a dead civilization. What stays untouched is "that foul cavern," the human heart. "Purify that inward sphere," Hawthorne writes, "and the many shapes of evil that haunt the outward, and which now seem almost our only realities, will turn to shadowy phantoms, and vanish of their own accord." Hawthorne, however, expected no such millennium, for what he saw lying in that dark cavern was human pride. Nathanael West likewise envisioned no millennium, and he too perceived that lying more deeply than fear and hate is pride— the pride that leads to a Hiroshima abroad and, when the locusts turn on each other, to a Waterloo at home. The Waterloo this time is not on some collapsing Hollywood set.

What West sees is the collapsing American myth of the open frontier, the tragedy of a society too proud to accept the disparity between promises and realities. It is in no way ironic that one of Miss Lonelyhearts' detractors should utter what may be the final truth in West's fiction, and the final significance of its journey theme, namely, that "we have no outer life, only an inner one, and that by necessity."

7

The Frontier
and Eschatology

I

Something eschatological is in the unforgettable scene that opens William Faulkner's *Light in August*. For four weeks Lena Grove, far along in pregnancy, has been journeying westward from her home in Alabama, searching for her lover, Lucas Burch, who has reneged on his promise to return. As she asks for his whereabouts, all the while with "unflagging and tranquil faith," her journey becomes "a long monotonous succession of peaceful and undeviating changes from day to dark and dark to day again," and the many wagons she rides in are "like something moving forever and without progress across an urn." The unhurried miles nevertheless unroll, and Lena draws ever closer to

Jefferson, where, on the day she sees it from the crest of the final hill, two columns of smoke rise. One comes from a coal stack, the other from Joanna Burden's burning house in which she lies murdered, her neck so deeply slashed that her head faces backwards. The smoke Lena sees from the distant hill portends the violence she will know once she leaves the pristine world behind her and enters civilized Jefferson. Smoke and fire signal the journey's end. They also forebode that "last ding-dong of doom" in that "last red and dying evening."[1]

Whether or not man prevails—and Faulkner of course insists he will—the concern with last things dominates Nathanael West's *The Day of the Locust,* this concern epitomized in Tod Hackett's canvas entitled "The Burning of Los Angeles." Other American titles evoke this same fascination: books like William Styron's *Set This House on Fire* and James Baldwin's *The Fire Next Time.* One thinks of the climactic burning in Henry James's *The Spoils of Poynton* or, in Hawthorne, not only of his story "Earth's Holocaust" but of those final words uttered by Ethan Brand: "Come deadly element of Fire. . . . Embrace me, as I do thee!" As between fire and ice, Robert Frost wryly resolves the eschatological question by joining "with those who favor fire."[2]

Inevitably the closed frontier becomes an eschatological matter. "What will America do—," asks Perry Miller, "what *can* America do—with an implacable prophecy that there is a point in time beyond which the very concept of a future becomes meaningless?"[3] This prophecy is Christian eschatology, brought to America by the Puritans who pondered *Revelation* and the words of Jesus in the Gospel of St. Luke: "I am come to send fire on the earth"; who had probably read again and again that line from John Donne's Holy Sonnet (Number 7): "All whom the flood did, and fire shall o'erthrow"; and who later knew Milton's *Paradise Lost,* especially its direful Books Two and Three. Even though they sought the fulfillment of a New Jerusalem, their vision necessarily committed them to a fiery apocalypse. This literal conflagration had nothing to do with America as such. Michael Wigglesworth's "The Day of Doom" described a universal fire. For all his spatial imagery the far more sophisticated symbolist Jonathan Edwards made the apocalypse something internal, an all-consuming hell of despair engulfing "the foolish children of men [who] miserably delude themselves in their own schemes, and in confidence in their own strength and wisdom."[4] Emblazoned though its imagery, Edwards' prophecy failed to hold eighteenth-century Americans who saw nothing cataclysmic to befall an already perfect order in nature and a perfectible order in mind. By the next century the notion of an attainable paradise fully discounted the prerequisite fire and brimstone. In the popular acceptance of unlimited progress, eschatology was irrelevant. Expansion westward put to rest all anxieties about either fire or ice. The illimitable frontier made the Christian prophecy seem absurd.

The question Perry Miller asked stems from what to an American is an even more fundamental question: "Can an errand, even an errand into the wilderness, be run indefinitely?"[5] Originally the errand was to establish a Biblical polity, a holy commonwealth in all matters both civil and ecclesiastical. Later generations, in filtering out the moral severity in this covenant, made the errand into something more social and economic—and utopian. Confident in their strength and wisdom, they easily filtered from their doctrine the human condition of sin. Or if the doctrine remained intact, the sinners, at least, disappeared. By the nineteenth century the utopian dream was far more American than Christian, primarily because eschatology had been expunged from it. Melville might describe the Galapagos Islands as once the scene of a great "penal conflagration," but the overtones bore no relation either to the American or to what had become his Edenic wilderness. Stronger than his involvement in nature was his effort to extricate himself from nature, to transcend finiteness and therefore eschatological limits. The open frontier was the perfect symbol for this American utopia.

This is why Frederick Jackson Turner's announcement of 1893 carries such shattering implications. Not only does it destroy the American Dream, but it brings back into the American consciousness what for two centuries had been denied. In those fateful words—"the frontier has gone"— concluding his famous essay, Turner revived the eschatological question upon which the Puritans had looked with both dread and fascination. It is the same question that nails down the adjective in *American* tragedy. To speculate about last things is to accept the possibility of limitation. To accept this possibility is to contemplate the end of the long American journey and to discover, with sudden abruptness, that as inheritors of Puritan theology we have been implicitly committed to this end from the beginning.

It is a different matter to speculate about T. S. Eliot's line, "In my end is my beginning,"[6] unless the point is that we begin to come of age when we end our illusions of infinite possibilities. Only initially is this Eliot's point, however, for his was a Christian position, one that committed him not only to human limitation but to divine salvation as well. Of course this is what Christian eschatology finally means: fire is itself a judgment, and from this judgment, as St. John spoke in *Revelation,* will come a new heaven and a new earth. But American tragedy stops short of this vision. That man will prevail is hardly to say he will know the millennium. What American tragedy does affirm is the closed frontier and the possibility that man will bring destructive fire upon himself. Thinking about Hiroshima, Perry Miller concludes his book on the Puritans' errand into the wilderness with the haunting reminder that "catastrophe, by and for itself, is not enough."[7] Miller does not suggest that catastrophe might be our redemptive beginning. To do so would be to take the leap of faith, just as making such a suggestion in this study of the closed frontier would be to go beyond tragedy.

II

Eleven years before the nineteenth century ended Mark Twain published *A Connecticut Yankee in King Arthur's Court,* and seven years into the new century Henry Adams privately published *The Education of Henry Adams.* The importance of both books is in how they made explicit what Frederick Jackson Turner only implied, if, indeed, he was even conscious of the eschatological implication that his 1893 essay carried. But the force with which this theme comes through in Twain and Adams makes clear that to both these writers the end of the century marked the *eschata* of history. They both foresaw catastrophe of national if not cosmic proportions, such that the apocalypse in Nathanael West's *The Day of the Locust* is merely a kind of validation for what had been seen half a century earlier.

Culminating in an Armageddon, *A Connecticut Yankee* does not concern the triumph of modern technology over medieval feudalism as much as it damns this same technology. The novel is less about the conflict of two civilizations as it is about American civilization itself, with the technology of destruction its hallmark. The real theme of the book is totally American; its structure, as Henry Nash Smith points out, brings into conflict two cultural symbols —the American Adam and the American Prometheus.[8] Hank Morgan, functioning as Mark Twain's Yankee, supposedly retains the American democratic ideals fostered by an earlier frontier society, even though he is the superintendent of the Colt arms factory in Hartford. In the novel he begins more as a representative of those agrarian values idealized by Cooper and Whitman than as someone transformed by closed, urban industrialism. But this was exactly Twain's problem. Could an Adam become a Prometheus? Could humane individualism function in a technological society? Could a Natty Bumppo superintend one of Andrew Carnegie's steel mills? Twain's answer is visualized in imagery of Armageddon. It was an answer costing Twain unspeakable anguish, for he had earlier believed in the American ideal of illimitable progress. That point when he irrevocably questioned this ideal was the same point at which he wrote *A Connecticut Yankee,* "a crisis so severe," writes Professor Smith, "that it led to an almost complete loss of control over his materials."[9] Nevertheless his answer was fixed, and in what was to be his last major novel Twain made clear that Adam had indeed become a Promethean monster, an extension of the machine and all its nonhuman imperatives. As if to prove to the rest of the world that American common sense and technology *must* triumph, and that those people sitting in darkness *must* be considered simply as the common enemy, Hank Morgan, the American Prometheus, carries out his errand with dynamite and Gatling guns, the nineteenth-century equivalent to napalm, M16s, and nuclear bombs.

But Morgan as The Boss does not conquer, even with twenty-five thousand enemy corpses around him. Disguised as a peasant woman who escaped the carnage, Merlin emerges to confirm what "Clarence," in the novel's postscript, already knows. Morgan and his fifty-three men are in a trap of their own making. If they stay in their defenses, the poisonous air bred by the surrounding mountains of dead will kill them. If they leave their fortifications, they will no longer be invincible. Like a Greek chorus pronouncing final doom, Merlin entones, "Ye were conquerors; ye are conquered."[10] He prophesies that all the transformed Connecticut Yankees will die, except The Boss, whom Merlin puts to sleep for thirteen centuries to reawaken in the late nineteenth century as testimony of total alienation from his Edenic heritage.

Twain saw that American democracy, at one time nurtured by frontier ideals, was now being changed into something inhuman and grotesque. The depth of his despair is indicated in the novel's last chapter, "The Battle of the Sand-Belt," a description of the kind of flawless killing that only modern technology can accomplish. With the efficiency of a computer, The Boss merely presses buttons to detonate hidden land mines that reduce thousands of the enemy to "homogeneous protoplasm, with alloys of iron and buttons." At the precise moment when thousands more advance among electrified wire fences, The Boss shoots current through all the fences, striking "the whole host dead in their tracks! *There* was a groan you could *hear!* It voiced the death-pang of eleven thousand men." The remainder—"perhaps ten thousand strong"—faced the Gatlings that "began to vomit death" into them. In back, the knights were trapped by a moat engineered to fill instantly. Halted by the "deluge of fire" in front, the enemy broke, turned about and "swept toward the ditch like chaff before a gale." Ten minutes completed the annihilation.

Reading through what Twain wrote in his last years explains why Bernard DeVoto, in discussing this period, entitled his essay "The Symbols of Despair."[11] Not only was Twain stricken with personal and financial tragedy, but questions about the nature of reality haunted him like a nightmare. Such stories as *The Mysterious Stranger,* "The Great Dark," "Which Was the Dream?" and "Which Was It?" supply his own frightful answers to questions he raises in his excoriating treatise *What Is Man?* (1904). Throughout these works a tone of impending disaster makes life and reality dreamlike. "Nothing exists," says Satan in *The Mysterious Stranger,* "save empty space—and you."

> It is true, that which I [Satan] have revealed to you; there is no God, no universe, no human race, no earthly life, no heaven, no hell. It is all a dream—a grotesque and foolish dream. Nothing exists but you. And you are but a *thought*—a vagrant thought, a useless thought, a homeless thought, wandering forlorn among the empty eternities![12]

Of the many "symbols of despair" in Twain's late writing, the burning of his family home occurred in both "Which Was the Dream?" and "Which Was It?" In two narrative fragments—"The Passenger's Story" and "The Enchanted Sea-Wilderness"—a burning ship served as an alternate symbol. The symbol of apocalyptic destruction stems from the fact that when in 1895 Twain revisited his old Hartford house, where he had lived during his seventeen most productive years, he imagined the event, according to John S. Tuckey, as a "homecoming fantasy," one in which he found himself "still at home with his family."[13] But his loss of fortune and, in 1896, of his daughter Susy through fatal meningitis served notice that his dream house was disastrously ruined. More than a symbol of disaster, it was for Twain a nightmarish symbol of despair, suggesting the end of everything. His nightmare was, in fact, his life.

That Twain yearned for a home forever lost but never forgotten compares with the horror with which he faced his own contemporary America. Under the crusading banner of imperialism, this America was not only the instrument of death abroad but, thoroughly deluded, the destroyer of its own frontier ideals at home. In the mass slaughter that ends *A Connecticut Yankee* and in the cold rationality with which this carnage is done, Twain's own fear, says Professor

Smith, "seems categorical and primal." For Twain rationality itself had become "a secularized version of Original Sin, and no means of redemption [was] in sight."[14] On such a fateful conclusion as this, Mark Twain rested his case against America.

III

What was violence in Mark Twain's eschatology was entropy in Henry Adams's. With despair both writers regarded America as lost.[15] To Twain this vision took on the quality of destruction, either an Armageddon with corpses piled mountain-high or a home burned to ashes. For Adams the chaos was silence, the inexorable dissipation of energy until, like a comet in the night sky, man disappears into the zero of darkness.

Broadly read in nineteenth-century science, Adams appropriated the so-called second law of thermodynamics to fashion his own eschatology. This law, made famous in the 1850s by the English physicists William Thomson and Lord Kelvin, states that mechanical energy in the material world is dissipating at such rate that within a finite time to come the earth will be uninhabitable. Contrary to Newtonian physics, this law denies the conservation of energy. Variously called the law of dissipation, the law of entropy, the law of degradation, it posits inevitable catastrophe as its central point. Its claims led astronomers to announce the death of the solar system, physicists the death of the sun, geologists the death of the earth, and anthropologists the death of the human race. In an effort to burst the superficial optimism of his own generation, Adams summarized the positions held by these nineteenth-century scientists. In his "Letter to American Teachers of History" (1910), for example, he quoted the geologist M. J. de Morgan, who asserted in 1909 that "the cold will return," that with the coming of glaciers populations will be pushed back into ever-smaller areas until, finding no more space, they "will be driven to internecine destruction."[16] Even more portentous was the announcement of M. Camille Flammarion, a noted astronomer, who described the time when "the last tribe, already expiring in cold and hunger, shall camp on the shores of the last sea in the rays of a pale sun which will henceforward illumine an earth that is only a wandering tomb, turning around a useless light and a barren heat."[17] The second law of thermodynamics provides man no escape. As a form of what Adams called "Vital Energy," man is "convicted of being a Vertebrate, a Mammal, a Monodelphe, a Primate." His flesh and blood condemn him to destruction; "science has shut and barred every known exit."[18]

All-importantly, Adams insisted that social energy was governed by the same law as physical energy. The historian, therefore, was as much a scientist as was a physicist. As such, Adams worked through one hypothesis after another to account for order and system in human affairs. Most notable are his essay "The Rule of Phase Applied to History" (1909) and such chapters as "The Grammar of Science," "A Dynamic Theory of History," and "A Law of Acceleration" in *The Education of Henry Adams*. What he passionately sought was some kind of synthesis, some all-embracing law to unify twentieth-century multiplicity. On the other hand, the giant dynamos he saw at the Chicago Exposition in 1893 convinced him that energy was chaotic. Symbolic of some awful and destructive power, they left him with "terror"[19] and, in a sense, sent him on a quest for an order that the dynamo served to negate. The colossal irony of this quest is that what Adams found as the central principle governing both the material and social world was nothing more than the principle of catastrophe.

The Education is the story of that foredoomed quest.

More than autobiography, the book is exactly what he called it: "A Study of Twentieth-Century Multiplicity."[20] Its immediate correlative was his own loss of faith in a singular order of existence. The values he inherited, while not directly attributable to the frontier, were based upon a moral order promising both human and social perfection. Such a moral law, he said, prepared him more for the year one than for the new century. *The Education* traces a lost traveler seeking meaning in a world stretching far beyond the power of his mind to understand.

Another correlative was America itself, especially its seething, post-Civil War capital of plotting politicians. The scandalous corner in gold organized by the stock gamblers Jay Gould and Jim Fisk, the madness of Charles Sumner in proposing the acquisition of Canada by the United States, the political character of President Grant (who was "archaic and should have lived in a cave and worn skins"), and the lesser corruption everywhere left Adams with no ideology to support. A traveler lost in his own country, he witnessed "the degradation of the democratic dogma," the title Brooks Adams later (1919) gave to the book that contained his brother's three essays—"The Tendency of History," "The Rule of Phase Applied to History," and "A Letter to American Teachers of History." Here in Washington, D.C., was ample evidence for Adams to conclude that the second law of thermodynamics applied to American political life. The end indeed seemed in sight. The fateful year 1893, when Turner announced the end of the frontier and when Adams saw the dynamos in Chicago, was also the year Adams read with much interest the manuscript of Brooks's *The Law of Civilization and Decay* (1895). For both brothers eschatology and history were fast becoming synonymous.

The substance most important in *The Education* is Adams's eschatological view of history. Throughout the book he was extraordinarily successful in sustaining dichotomies—mind and matter, chaos and order, unity and diversity, youth and age, even winter and summer. But his artful synthesis ironically calls attention to the fact that any other synthesis except the one foreboding entropy and death was not for Adams to have. The book powerfully depicts failure—the failure of Adams, the protagonist, to achieve a vision of unity all men dream of. In his "A Letter to American Teachers of History" he called this dream "the most deceptive of all the innumerable illusions of the mind"; as an idea it "survives the idea of God or of Universe; it is innate and intuitive."[21] In *The Education,* one of America's great literary tragedies, Adams, the dreamer, confronts the inevitability of last things. Not only does he discover that "chaos was the law of nature" and order "the dream of man"; he also finds the mind "looking blankly into the void of death." The inexorable processes of history take one to this final and inevitable end. The frontier is closed. Even the mind offers no escape. One's vital energies, like those of the universe, decline and die. Failure to transcend this destiny must necessarily be total failure. R. P. Blackmur calls Adams's failure "genuine." Intended as an encomium of greatness, this kind of failure "comes hard and slow, and, as in a tragedy, is only fully realized at the end."[22]

IV

Even the briefest survey of nineteenth-century American literature indicates that the cosmic optimism of Emerson, Thoreau, and Whitman did not carry the day. While Emerson in "Circles" confidently asserted that the soul knows no boundary, that "the heart refuses to be imprisoned," and that "there is no outside, no inclosing wall, no circumference to us," Poe was describing in *Eureka* the annihilation of the universe and the entropy of mind. Thoreau, who understood the art of walking as something holy—a Saunterer was a Holy-Lander—took his direction westward where, he says in "Walking," he can go as a free man. In this direction "the nation is moving," and, he adds, "mankind progresses from east to west." Hawthorne, on the other hand, regarded flight, whether east or west, as delusion; in *The House of the Seven Gables* this wisdom is Hepzibah's when, pausing with Clifford on their brief but exhilarating train ride, she kneels on the station platform and prays to God: "Have mercy on us!" Whitman, the third member of the American triad, wrote Emerson a letter with a complimentary copy of his new testament, *Leaves of Grass*: "Master, I am a man who has perfect faith. Master, we have not come through centuries, caste, heroisms, fables, to halt in this land today."[23] By contrast, walls meant everything to Melville: walls enclosing Bartleby and Pierre, walls along the terrible Liverpool streets, chapel walls in which were masoned memorial tablets with black borders, and the most terrifying wall—the whale's head, a "dead, blind wall."

That notions of infinite progression did not carry the day is simply a result of their being intolerable to a Poe, a Hawthorne, and a Melville—and to all persons who recognize the tragic clash between illusion and reality. This is why students of American literature would do well to read R. W. B. Lewis's *The American Adam* and Harry Levin's *The Power of Blackness*. Side by side the two books show nineteenth-century American writers struggling over this dichotomy symbolized by light and darkness and extended to mythic dimensions. This allusive range encompasses infinite creation as well as finite restriction, innocence as well as tragedy. The vision of one stimulates the sense of the other, just as an alpha implies an omega.

By the end of the century these clashing ideas took steadfast forms. On the one hand, the determinists saw life as nothing more than a mechanical problem. With such terms as "natural selection," "biochemical processes," "conditioned reflex," and "Archaeozoic Age," they created a world-view founded on an unyielding mechanical determinism. Their authorities were Charles Darwin and Thomas Henry Huxley, Auguste Comte and Herbert Spencer, Ivan Pavlov and Sigmund Freud, Sir Francis Galton and Sir James Frazer. The outcome in American literature was a *Maggie* (1893), a *MacTeague* (1899), and a *Sister Carrie* (1900). On the other hand, the New Thought movement, growing out from the Neo-Hegelians in St. Louis and certain Eastern mystics, claimed that the naturalistic world of physical force only hid the real world of mind and spirit. This movement led to Christian Science and the widespread popularity of Theosophy, Spiritualism, other occult groups, and psychical research. Early inquirers included Orestes Brownson and Margaret Fuller; but as the century waned, many more American writers were asking if cosmic consciousness were indeed the new frontier. Oliver Wendell Holmes in *Elsie Venner* (1861), Edward Bellamy in *Looking Backward* (1880), and William Dean Howells in *The Undiscovered Country* (1880), *The Shadow of a Dream* (1890), and *Questionable Shapes* (1903), were all concerned with occult transcendence. To many Americans Eastern mysticism and, more specifically, Buddhism, offered the answer to a closed, materialistic world with its new science. Percival Lowell wrote *The Soul of the Far East* (1888); John LaFarge, who traveled to the South Seas and Japan with Henry Adams in 1890, wrote *An Artist's Letters from Japan* (1897); William Sturgis Bigelow, *Buddhism and Immortality* (1908); Lafcadio Hearn, a long series of volumes about Japan, where he had exiled himself.

The metaphor of the frontier relates to these conflicting ideas. An open frontier came to mean a new existence, a rebirth, enabling man to transcend space and time, mortality and death. Intimations of this new level of existence were supposedly evident to persons who had freed themselves from a materialistic or entropic world-view. The whole New Thought movement endeavored to explain divine essence and its force in human affairs. It sought a new species of man. As perhaps to be expected, it was to California that Annie Besant, successor to Madame Blavatsky as international head of the Theosophical Society, went in 1926 to supervise the newly gathered members of this new species in the name of Theosophy.

Most sensational of New Thought efforts to cross the metaphoric frontier was the investigation of extrasensory capacities. In *Forty Years of Psychic Research* (1936) and *The Mystery of the Buried Crosses: A Narrative of Psychic Exploration* (1939) Hamlin Garland documented his longtime psychical interests, which had begun when he wrote *Tyranny of the Dark* (1905) and *The Shadow World* (1908). Higher consciousness, telepathy, precognition, spiritualism —what it all comes to, as Rosalind Heywood tells in *Beyond the Reach of Sense,* is the belief that a person can make contact with distant events or with supraphenomena by a process not involving sight, hearing, touch, taste, or smell. Such miraculous inventions as the telephone and telegraph encouraged people's curiosities about thought transmission, especially between the living and the dead. Thomas A. Edison tried to make "a sort of valve" to allow "personalities in another existence" to have a "better opportunity to express themselves than the tilting tables and raps and ouija boards and mediums and other crude methods now purported to be the only means of communication."[24] The year before Edison announced his intention, Francis Grierson devised a "psycho-phone" to use during his lectures to the Toronto Theosophical Society in 1919. This "phone," effecting intercourse between this world and the next, brought messages that Grierson recorded in *Psycho-Phone Messages* (1921). Garland boasted that Los Angeles mediums whom he knew had received messages from the spirits of Henry James, Sir Arthur Conan Doyle, Walt Whitman, and others. Edith Ellis in *Open the Door* (1935) reported contact with Madame Blavatsky, Abraham Lincoln, the Virgin Mary, and Jesus Christ!

One way of escaping nineteenth-century conventions was to go west, another way was to go "beyond." Nothing was too bizarre to keep frontiers open. The American's hunger for being—and becoming still more—inclined him toward those irresistible words spoken by the serpent to Adam and Eve: "Ye shall be as gods!" The metaphor of the closed frontier eclipses these words. It mocks human efforts to reach beyond the grave. It confronts one with the essentials of *this* life and then promises nothing more. The closed frontier, in short, is the foundation of tragedy. It makes certain that one will never become what he envisions.

These are harsh conditions for a nation whose myths have allowed no room for failure. The open frontier with all its attendant pride has been the context for foreign policy since the eighteenth century; in the present century frontierism has influenced American action at Versailles, Yalta, and Nuremburg. The same kind of "Diplomacy in Eden"[25] incinerates Vietnamese. This militant innocence is behind what J. William Fulbright calls "arrogance of power." "Once imbued with the idea of mission," he writes, "a great nation easily assumes that it has the means as well as the duty to do God's will."[26] Unfortunately, arrogance prepares no nation to accept its limitations, even though, as Fulbright adds, history makes it clear that the world has endured all it can of crusading, "high-minded men bent on the regeneration of the human race."[27] A nation understanding the lessons of tragedy knows the difference between contemplating God and playing God, between accepting limitation and rebelling against it. The lessons to be learned fill literature and history. But, perversely, men and nations prefer their own death to that of their illusions.

This is the eschatological consequence of pride. An end to human affairs comes when we forget that these affairs are only human. To confront this humanness is the anxiety of our having to be in the world with no exit. The condition is both psychological and ontological. It is this latter dimension that the metaphor of the closed frontier finally touches. The wall makes escape impossible, and we are left to face guilt and terror, life and death.

Santayana once observed that the American has never had "to face the trials of Job." What would his attitude be, Santayana wondered, "if serious and irremediable tribulation ever overtook him."[28] For all the violence and hatred overtaking him, the American may yet not recognize, let alone accept, the more tragic condition that what he sees he cannot be. As J. D. Salinger's Holden Caulfield said, such a person still wants to grab for the golden ring. Only after he has reached for it and fallen will he ask Job's agonizing question: "Why is light given to a man whose way is hid, and whom God hath hedged in?"

Notes

CHAPTER 1

1. T. S. Eliot, *The Family Reunion,* in *The Complete Poems and Plays, 1909–1950* (New York, 1952), p. 242.
2. Stephen E. Whicher (ed.), *Selections from Ralph Waldo Emerson* (Boston, 1960), p. 253.
3. Edwin Fussell, *Frontier: American Literature and the American West* (Princeton, N.J., 1965), pp. 285–291.
4. Fussell, p. 394.

CHAPTER 2

1. Unless otherwise noted, all quotations from Turner are taken from Ray Allen Billington (ed.), *Frontier and*

Section: *Selected Essays of Frederick Jackson Turner* (Englewood Cliffs, N.J., 1961).

2. Benjamin W. F. Wright, Jr., "Political Institutions and the Frontier," in Dixon Ryan Fox (ed.), *Sources of Culture in the Middle West: Backgrounds versus Frontier* (New York, 1934), p. 16.
3. Merle Curti, *Probing Our Past* (New York, 1955), p. 32.
4. John C. Almack, "The Shibboleth of the Frontier," *The Historical Outlook,* XVI (May 1925), 197.
5. Wright, pp. 34–35.
6. A. O. Craven, "Frederick Jackson Turner," in William T. Hutchinson (ed.), *The Marcus W. Jernegan Essays in American Historiography* (New York, 1958), p. 264.
7. Henry Nash Smith, *Virgin Land: The American West as Symbol and Myth* (Cambridge, Mass., 1950), p. 297.
8. Karl Shapiro, "Why Out-Russia Russia?" *New Republic,* 138 (June 9, 1958), 12.
9. Arthur M. Schlesinger, Jr., "The Historian as Artist," *Atlantic Monthly,* CCXII (July 1963), 38.
10. Carl L. Becker, *Everyman His Own Historian: Essays on History and Politics* (New York, 1935), pp. 191–232.
11. Fred J. Turner, "The Poet of the Future," *University [of Wisconsin] Press* (1883), 4–6.
12. Smith, p. 298.
13. Craven, in Fox, p. 40.
14. Louis M. Hacker, "Sections—or Classes?" *The Nation,* CXXXVII (July 26, 1933), 108.
15. Paul Tillich, *The Interpretation of History* (New York, 1936), p. 96.

CHAPTER 3

1. Ray Allen Billington (ed.), "Introduction," in Frederick Jackson Turner, *Frontier and Section* (Englewood Cliffs, N.J., 1961), p. 6.

2. Perry Miller, *Errand into the Wilderness* (Cambridge, Mass., 1956).

3. Quoted in Charles L. Sanford, *The Quest for Paradise* (Urbana, Ill., 1961), pp. 82–83.

4. R. W. B. Lewis, *The American Adam: Innocence, Tragedy, and Tradition in the Nineteenth Century* (Chicago, 1955), chap. 7.

5. The Emerson and Whitman quotations are from "The American Scholar" and "Passage to India" respectively.

6. Sanford, p. vi.

7. D. H. Lawrence, *Studies in Classic American Literature* (New York, 1953), p. 64; J. Frank Dobie, *The Longhorns* (Boston, 1941), pp. 41–42.

8. See Henry Nash Smith, *Virgin Land* (Cambridge, Mass., 1950), chap. 16; Henry Steele Commager, *The American Mind* (New Haven, 1950), p. 41; Henry F. May, *The End of American Innocence* (New York, 1959); Van Wyck Brooks, *New England Indian Summer, 1865–1915* (New York, 1940); Leo Marx, *The Machine in the Garden: Technology and the Pastoral Ideal in America* (New York, 1964).

9. Ralph Waldo Emerson, "Nature."

10. Henry David Thoreau, "Civil Disobedience."

11. Mary Baker Eddy, *Science and Health with Key to the Scripture* (Boston, n. d.), p. 468.

12. Miguel de Unamuno, *Tragic Sense of Life,* trans. J. E. Crawford Flinch (New York, 1954), pp. 38–39.

13. George Santayana, *Winds of Doctrine* (New York, 1913), p. 191.

14. Robert Frost, "A Considerable Speck."

15. Max Wylie, "Aspects of E. G. O. (Eugene Gladstone O'Neill)," *The Carrell,* II (June 1961), 1–12.

16. Charles T. Michener, "The Spectre of Suicide," *Seattle,* III (March 1966), 34–40.

17. James Reston in *The New York Times* (July 16, 1964), p. 16.

18. Daniel J. Boorstin, *The Image: or What Happened to the American Dream* (New York, 1962), p. 6.

19. Carl Jung, *Modern Man in Search of a Soul* (New York, 1933), p. 108.

20. Van Wyck Brooks, *America's Coming of Age* (New York, 1958), p. 78.

21. Joseph Wood Krutch, *The Modern Temper* (New York, 1929), chap. 5.

22. Arthur Miller, "Tragedy and the Common Man," in Robert W. Corrigan (ed.), *Tragedy: Vision and Form* (San Francisco, 1965), p. 150.

23. Reinhold Niebuhr, *The Nature and Destiny of Man,* I (New York, 1941), p. 181.

24. William Faulkner, *Faulkner in the University,* eds. Frederick L. Gwynn and Joseph L. Blotner (New York, 1965), p. 26.

25. Joseph Campbell, *Hero with a Thousand Faces* (New York, 1956), p. 11.

26. James B. Conant, *Modern Science and Modern Man* (New York, 1952), pp. 70, 86–87.

27. Percy W. Bridgman, *The Way Things Are* (Cambridge, Mass., 1959), p. 6.

28. J. Robert Oppenheimer, *The Open Mind* (New York, 1955), p. 54.

29. Quoted in Herbert J. Muller, *The Spirit of Tragedy* (New York, 1956), p. 5.

30. David L. Stevenson, "The Activists," *Daedalus,* (Spring 1963), 241.

CHAPTER 4

1. Henry Nash Smith, *Mark Twain: The Development of a Writer* (Cambridge, Mass., 1962), pp. 114, 124, 137.

2. T. S. Eliot, "Introduction," *Huckleberry Finn* (New York, 1950), pp. ix, xv.

3. Richard Chase, *The American Novel and Its Tradition* (New York, 1957), pp. 148, 144.

4. James M. Cox, "Remarks on the Sad Initiation of Huckleberry Finn," *Sewanee Review,* LXII (Summer 1954), 394.
5. William C. Spengemann, *Mark Twain and the Backwoods Angel: The Matter of Innocence in the Works of Samuel L. Clemens* (Kent, Ohio, 1966), p. 131.
6. W. R. Moses, "The Pattern of Evil in *Adventures of Huckleberry Finn,*" *The Georgia Review,* XIII (Summer 1959), 166.
7. Van Wyck Brooks, *The Ordeal of Mark Twain* (New York, 1920); Justin Kaplan, *Mr. Clemens and Mark Twain: A Biography* (New York, 1966).
8. See Walter Blair, *Mark Twain & Huck Finn* (Berkeley, 1960), chaps. 11–13; also "When Was *Huckleberry Finn* Written?" *American Literature,* XXX (March 1958), 1–25. Regarding Twain's inconsiderate speech at John Greenleaf Whittier's seventieth birthday celebration (December 17, 1877), see Blair, pp. 155–158.
9. Leo Marx, "Mr. Eliot, Mr. Trilling, and *Huckleberry Finn,*" *American Scholar,* XXII (Autumn 1953), 440.
10. All quoted references to *The Adventures of Huckleberry Finn* come from the 1948 (New York) edition, with Introduction by Lionel Trilling.
11. Philip Young, *Ernest Hemingway* (New York, 1952), pp. 190–191.
12. Henry Nash Smith and William M. Gibson (eds.), *Mark Twain–Howells Letters,* I (Cambridge, Mass., 1960), pp. 91–92.
13. Smith, p. 119.
14. Donna Gerstenberger, "Huckleberry Finn and the World's Illusions," *The Western Humanities Review,* XIV (Autumn 1960), 401, 403.
15. Quoted in Blair, p. 289.
16. Carlos Baker, *Hemingway: The Writer as Artist* (Princeton, N.J., 1963), pp. 180–181. Although Baker does not allege influence, he tellingly compares the prose opening Chapter 19 of *Huckleberry Finn* and Chapter 31 of *A Farewell to Arms.*

17. Gladys Carmen Bellamy, *Mark Twain as a Literary Artist* (Norman, Okla., 1950), p. 340.
18. Cox, 398.
19. Randall Stewart, *American Literature and Christian Doctrine* (Baton Rouge, 1950), p. 121.
20. Floyd Stovall, *American Idealism* (Norman, Okla., 1943), p. 103.
21. Karl Jaspers, *Tragedy Is Not Enough* (Boston, 1952), p. 42.
22. Northrop Frye, *Anatomy of Criticism* (Princeton, N.J., 1957), p. 213.
23. Albert Bigelow Paine (ed.), *Mark Twain's Notebook* (New York, 1935), p. 212.

CHAPTER 5

1. *Their Fathers' God,* trans. Trygve M. Ager (New York, 1931), pp. 234, 235.
2. Theodore Jorgenson and Nora.O. Solum, *Ole Edvart Rölvaag: A Biography* (New York, 1939), p. 26.
3. Quoted in Jorgenson and Solum, p. 39.
4. Jorgenson and Solum, p. 167.
5. O. E. Rölvaag, "The Vikings of the Middle West," *American Magazine,* CVIII (October 1929), 47.
6. *Giants in the Earth: A Saga of the Prairies,* trans. Lincoln Colcord (New York, 1927), p. 111.
7. Joseph E. Baker, "Western Man Against Nature: *Giants in the Earth,*" *College English,* IV (October 1942), 19–26.
8. Pascal's *Pensées,* 347.
9. Percy H. Boynton, "O. E. Rölvaag and the Conquest of the Pioneer," *English Journal,* XVIII (September 1929), 535–542.
10. Boynton, 536–537.
11. Vernon Louis Parrington, "Editor's Introduction," *Giants in the Earth* (New York, 1929), p. xvii.
12. Henry Steele Commager, "The Literature of the Pio-

neer West," *Minnesota History,* VIII (March 1942), 319, 326.

13. *Peder Victorious,* trans. Nora O. Solum (New York, 1929), p. 325.
14. George Santayana, *Interpretations of Poetry and Religion* (New York, 1957), p. 178.
15. Paul M. Reigstad, *The Art and Mind of O. E. Rölvaag,* unpublished Ph.D. dissertation (Albuquerque, 1958), p. 204.
16. Quoted in Baker, 23.
17. Quoted in Reigstad, p. 206.
18. Jorgenson and Solum, pp. 265–266.
19. Quoted in Jorgenson and Solum, pp. 276–277.
20. Theodore Jorgenson, "The Main Factors in Rölvaag's Authorship," *Norwegian-American Studies and Records,* X (1938), 146.
21. John Neitmann, "Ole Edvart Rölvaag," *Norwegian-American Studies and Records,* XII (1941), 157–158.
22. Jorgenson, 148.
23. Quoted in Einar I. Haugen, "O. E. Rölvaag: Norwegian-American," *Norwegian-American Studies and Records,* VII (1933), 62.
24. Quoted in Reigstad, p. 109.
25. Quoted in Jorgenson and Solum, p. 323.
26. *Boat of Longing,* trans. Nora O. Solum (New York, 1933), p. 243.
27. Parrington, p. ix.
28. Quoted in Jorgenson and Solum, pp. 155–156.
29. Quoted letter to Percy H. Boynton, in Reigstad, pp. 210–211.
30. Commager, 327.

CHAPTER 6

1. Quoted in Ray Allen Billington, *The Far Western Frontier* (New York, 1962), p. 149.
2. Quoted in Billington, p. 149.

3. Edmund Wilson, *The Boys in the Back Room: Notes on California Novelists* (San Francisco, 1941), p. 63.
4. Bayard Taylor, *Eldorado: or Adventures in the Path of Empire,* intro. Robert Glass Cleland (New York, 1949), p. 97.
5. Billington, *America's Frontier Heritage* (New York, 1966), p. 26.
6. Zane Grey, "Breaking Through: The Story of My Life," *The American Magazine,* 98 (July 1924), 80.
7. Franklin Walker, *A Literary History of Southern California* (Berkeley, 1950), p. 231.
8. Walker, p. 231.
9. Paul Jordan-Smith, "Los Angeles: Ballyhooers in Heaven," from Duncan Aikman (ed.), *The Taming of the Frontiers* (New York, 1925), p. 285.
10. *Religious Bodies: 1926* (Government Printing Office, 1930), pp. 457–459; *Los Angeles, a Guide to the City and Its Environs,* American Guide Series (New York, 1941), pp. 68–73.
11. Jordan-Smith, pp. 271, 279.
12. Stanley Edgar Hyman, *Nathanael West* (Minneapolis, 1962), p. 27.
13. James F. Light, *Nathanael West: An Interpretive Study* (Evanston, 1961); Angel Flores, "Miss Lonelyhearts in the Haunted Castle," *Contempo,* III (July 25, 1933), 1; Victor Comerchero, *Nathanael West: The Ironic Prophet* (Seattle, 1967); Nathanael West, "Some Notes on Miss L.," *Contempo,* III (May 15, 1933), 2.
14. Randall Reid, *The Fiction of Nathanael West: No Redeemer, No Promised Land* (Chicago, 1968), pp. 141–144.
15. David D. Galloway, "Nathanael West's Dream Dump," *Critique: Studies in Modern Fiction,* VI (Winter 1963), 60–61.
16. Wilson, p. 72.
17. Comerchero, p. 51.
18. Quoted in Light, p. 69.
19. All subsequent references to West's novels are taken

from *A Cool Million* and *The Dream Life of Balso Snell,* both novels in one volume (New York, 1965); and *Miss Lonelyhearts* and *The Day of the Locust,* both novels also in one volume (New York, 1962). The four novels are available in one volume, *The Complete Works of Nathanael West* (New York, 1957).

20. Herman Melville, *Pierre, or The Ambiguities* (New York, 1949), pp. 247–253.
21. Thomas M. Lorch, "West's Miss Lonelyhearts: Skepticism Mitigated?" *Renascence,* XVIII (Winter 1966), 99–109; "Religion and Art in *Miss Lonelyhearts,"* *Renascence,* XX (Autumn 1967), 11–17.
22. West, "Some Notes on Miss L.," 2.
23. Lorch, "Religion and Art," 12.
24. Daniel Aaron, " 'The Truly Monstrous': A Note on Nathanael West," *Partisan Review,* XIV (January–February 1947), 98–106.
25. V. L. Lokke, "A Side Glance at Medusa: Hollywood, the Literature Boys, and Nathanael West," *Southwest Review,* XLVI (Winter 1961), 42.
26. Aaron, "Waiting for the Apocalypse," *The Hudson Review,* III (Winter 1951), 634.
27. Letter from West to Jack Conway, quoted in Richard Gehman's introduction to *The Day of the Locust* (New York, 1950), pp. ix–x.
28. Reid, p. 154.
29. West, "Some Notes on Violence," *Contact,* I (October 1932), 132.
30. Frederick J. Hoffman, *The Mortal No: Death and the Modern Imagination* (Princeton, N.J., 1964), p. 141.

CHAPTER 7

1. William Faulkner, *Light in August* (New York, 1950), p. 6; "Address Upon Receiving the Nobel Prize for Literature," in *The Portable Faulkner,* revised edition (New York, 1967), p. 724.

2. Nathaniel Hawthorne, "Ethan Brand," in *The Novels and Tales of Nathaniel Hawthorne* (New York, 1937), p. 1195; Robert Frost, "Fire and Ice," in *Complete Poems of Robert Frost* (New York, 1964), p. 268. See also R. W. B. Lewis's discussion of American apocalyptic literature in "Days of Wrath and Laughter," *Trials of the Word: Essays in American Literature and the Humanistic Tradition* (New Haven, 1965), pp. 184–235.

3. Perry Miller, *Errand into the Wilderness* (New York, 1956), p. 217.

4. Jonathan Edwards, "Sinners in the Hands of an Angry God," in Clarence H. Faust and Thomas H. Johnson (eds.), *Jonathan Edwards* (New York, 1962), p. 160.

5. Miller, p. 217.

6. T. S. Eliot, *Four Quartets* (New York, 1943), p. 17.

7. Miller, p. 239.

8. Henry Nash Smith, *Mark Twain's Fable of Progress: Political and Economic Ideas in "A Connecticut Yankee"* (New Brunswick, N.J., 1964), p. 104; see also "The Fall of Prometheus" in Roger B. Salomon, *Twain and the Image of History* (New Haven, 1961).

9. Smith, pp. 94–95.

10. Mark Twain, *A Connecticut Yankee in King Arthur's Court* (New York, 1899), p. 404.

11. In Bernard DeVoto, *Mark Twain at Work* (Cambridge, Mass., 1942).

12. Mark Twain, *The Mysterious Stranger,* in *The Portable Mark Twain* (New York, 1946), pp. 743–744.

13. Mark Twain, *Which Was the Dream? and Other Symbolic Writings of the Later Years,* ed. John S. Tuckey (Berkeley, 1967), p. 5.

14. Smith, p. 107.

15. See Tony Tanner, "The Lost America—The Despair of Henry Adams and Mark Twain," in *Mark Twain: A Collection of Critical Essays* (Englewood Cliffs, N.J., 1963), pp. 159–174.

16. Henry Adams, *The Degradation of the Democratic Dogma* (New York, 1958), pp. 177–178.

17. Adams, pp. 178–179.
18. Adams, p. 187.
19. Henry Adams, *Henry Adams and His Friends: A Collection of His Unpublished Letters,* ed. Harold Dean Cater (Boston, 1947), p. 292.
20. Henry Adams, *The Education of Henry Adams* (Boston, 1918), p. 435.
21. Adams, *The Degradation,* p. 238.
22. R. P. Blackmur, *The Expense of Greatness* (Gloucester, Mass., 1958), p. 255.
23. Walt Whitman, *Leaves of Grass,* Comprehensive Readers' Edition, eds. Harold W. Blodgett and Sculley Bradley (New York, 1965), p. 731.
24. Dagobert D. Runes (ed.), *The Diary and Sundry Observations of Thomas Alva Edison* (New York, 1948), p. 239.
25. Charles L. Sanford, *The Quest for Paradise* (Urbana, Ill., 1961), chap. 12.
26. J. William Fulbright, *The Arrogance of Power* (New York, 1967), p. 4.
27. Fulbright, p. 248.
28. George Santayana, *Character and Opinion in the United States* (New York, 1956), p. 116.

Index